MAGIC OF A
MYSTIC

PADRE PIO AS A YOUNG MAN SHORTLY
AFTER HIS ORDINATION.

MAGIC OF A MYSTIC

MYSTIC

◆ STORIES ◆ OF ◆
PADRE PIO

THE DUCHESS OF ST. ALBANS

Clarkson N. Potter, Inc./Publishers
DISTRIBUTED BY CROWN PUBLISHERS, INC., NEW YORK

We GRATEFULLY ACKNOWLEDGE PERMISSION TO REPRINT THE FOLLOWING:

Pages 21, 69, 137, 146: Passages taken from *The Friar of San Giovanni: Tales of Padre Pio*, by John McCaffery, published and copyright © 1980 by Darton, Longman and Todd Limited, London. Reprinted by permission of the publisher.

Pages 50, 52: Extracts from Padre Pio's letters in *Padre Pio, His Life and Mission*, by Mary Ingoldsby, published by Veritas Publications, Dublin, Ireland. Reprinted by permission.

Page 70: The conversation between Padre Pio and Dr. Sanguinetti from *Padre Pio: The Stigmatist*, by Charles Mortimer Carty, published by TAN Books & Publishers, Inc. Reprinted by permission of the publisher.

Page 144: Portions of Padre Pio's inauguration speech reprinted by permission of "Voce di Padre Pio," Convento S. Maria delle Grazie, San Giovanni Rotondo, Italy.

Page 164: Excerpt from *Needles of Stone*, by Tom Graves, published by The Turnstone Press, London, and reprinted by permission.

Pages 22–25, 37: Biographical material from *Padre Pio, Childhood and Adolescence*, by Gherardo Leone, by permission of the author and La Casa Sollievo della Sofferenza, San Giovanni Rotondo, Italy.

Copyright © 1983 by Suzanne St. Albans

Published by Clarkson N. Potter, Inc.,
One Park Avenue, New York, New York 10016,
and simultaneously in Canada
by General Publishing Company Limited

Manufactured in the United States of America

Library of Congress Cataloging in Publication Data

St. Albans, Suzanne Marie Adèle Beauclerk, Duchess of.
Magic of a mystic.

1. Pio, Padre, 1887–1968. 2. Catholic Church—
Italy—Biography. I. Title.
BX4705.P49S7 1983 271'.36'024 [B] 82-19084
ISBN 0-517-54847-X

The text of this book is set in Palatino.
Design by Gael Towey Dillon
Maps by Lynne Arany

10 9 8 7 6 5 4 3 2 1
First Edition

Give me a good digestion, Lord,
And also something to digest;
But when and how that something comes
I leave to thee who knowest best.

Give me a healthy body, Lord,
Give me the sense to keep it so;
Also a heart that is not bored
Whatever work I have to do.

Give me a healthy mind, Good Lord,
That finds the good that dodges sight;
And seeing sin, is not appalled,
But seeks a way to put it right.

Give me a point of view, Good Lord,
Let me know what it is and why.
Don't let me worry overmuch
About the thing that's known as "I."

Give me a sense of humor, Lord,
Give me the power to see a joke,
To get some happiness from life
And pass it on to other folk.

This prayer, which is often erroneously attributed to Sir Thomas More, was written by Thomas Henry Basil Webb, born August 12, 1898, and killed on the Somme, December 1, 1917, age nineteen.

CONTENTS

PADRO PIO LOVED CHILDREN, WHOSE INNOCENCE HE AL-
WAYS TRIED TO FOSTER IN HIS OWN DISCIPLES.

PREFACE

LTHOUGH HE RARELY STEPPED OUT OF HIS OWN FRI-
ary of Santa Maria delle Grazie, Padre Pio was the
center of life in the southern Italian town of San
Giovanni Rotondo during the entire fifty years of his
apostolate.

The fascination of his gruff manner and the magne-
tism of his extraordinary saintliness drew people to him,
and once they had met him, the experience marked them
for life. The only way to talk to him personally and pri-
vately was through the medium of confession. There he
listened, admonished, advised, encouraged and thundered in turn.

When I first began talking to people who had known
him well, I feared that his influence had prevailed mostly
upon women. But when I met his male friends, spiritual
sons and disciples, I realized that thousands of men came
to see him from all over the world—exalted church digni-
taries, eminent statesmen, scientists and professional
men of every kind. Although he never read a newspaper
or listened to the radio, he could discuss world affairs
and all erudite subjects with his most learned visitors.

This is not a biography of Padre Pio. It is a collection
of stories as told to me by people who knew him well.
Certain points of his life, such as the persecutions and his

death, will inevitably come up many times. I have deliberately retained some of the repetitions to show how these events affected each individual, according to his or her sensitivity and degree of spiritual awareness. In this way I hope that a picture of the real, living Padre Pio, whom I never met, will emerge.

I would like to thank Father Joseph Pius for his kind help and assistance during the writing of this book. The often humorous cooperation of the people of San Giovanni was also invaluable, and although we sometimes started off on a somewhat cautious and wary footing, we usually ended up good friends.

Elidé, wonderful Elidé, kept my spirits afloat whenever they threatened to dive out of sight. "It's the devil who is putting these ideas into your head," she said vigorously, every time doubts about writing a book of this kind overwhelmed me. Her own indomitable faith always made short work of the devil's attacks on herself.

My wholehearted gratitude goes to my sister Christine for her constant urging and prodding, for persuading reluctant individuals to open up, and for soothing natural suspicions and arranging difficult interviews. She unearthed old forgotten facts and translated and interpreted whenever my own limited knowledge of Italian failed me. She also took many of the photographs herself, and collected the rest from various sources.

And last but not least, I must thank her for making sure that I was decently attired before setting out from her house every day. "You will get lynched if you go out like that," she remarked severely as she caught me slinking out of her garden early one magic summer morning in skintight jeans and sleeveless T-shirt. Fresh from the beaches of the south of France, I was an innocent abroad, unaware that some of the holy women of San Giovanni take it upon themselves to enforce modesty of dress in the streets. "If you meet so-and-so she will probably box your ears or give you a sharp poke in the ribs. And then there is what's-her-name, who goes around with a cat-o'-nine-tails for flicking bare arms and legs. I wouldn't risk it if I were you. . . ."

And this was my introduction to Padre Pio's extraordinary "children."

MAGIC OF A
MYSTIC

THE FRIARY AND CHURCH OF SANTA MARIA DELLE GRAZIE
AS THEY APPEARED WHEN PADRE PIO FIRST ARRIVED IN 1916.

· 1 ·

THE FOUNDER'S
FEAST DAY

A DEAFENING DETONATION JOLTS ME AWAKE. I SIT UP
in bed in alarm. The sky is milky white, which
means that the sun must be about to rise. Then
more explosions rumble through the still air, and Mini,
the little white terrier, sets up a howl.

"Don't worry," shouts my sister Christine from her
bedroom, "it's only the friars blasting off their fireworks."

The celebrations marking the eighth centenary of the
birth of Saint Francis of Assisi are starting off with a
bang. In southern Italy, this is the way the faithful honor
their saints. As the Little Poor Man of Assisi is both the
patron saint of Padre Pio and the founder of the Franciscan order, this is going to be a great day.

There will clearly be no more sleeping this morning,
so I shuffle over to Christine's bedroom. She is on her
knees, cooing soothingly to Mini, who quivers like a
blancmange under the bed. Her house, huddled under
the walls of the friary gardens, receives the full force of
the rockets' blast.

Christine first visited Santa Maria delle Grazie in San
Giovanni Rotondo, a remote town in the Gargano Moun-

1

tains, in the last years of Padre Pio's life, and her one wish from then on was to come back. As soon as she was able to rearrange her life, she made straight for the Gargano with the firm intention of buying a house. But this, she was informed, was an impossible dream. In the throes of galloping development, the little town was brimming with souls in search of salvation, followed, as is usual in such cases, by a retinue of parasites. So every dwelling was occupied, and nothing ever came up for sale.

In spite of the hopelessness of it all, she brought up the subject when she stopped at the hotel for coffee before going back to Rome. And although she got the expected reply, she left her Rome telephone number with the barman all the same.

The next day, to her amazement, there was a call from him. Half an hour after her departure, a woman had come in and asked if he knew of anyone who wanted to buy "a small house with a small garden." The very words she had used herself! So back she came at once, met the owner, and bought the place outright.

The house was in bad repair. Gradually my sister put it in order, and when her new home was finally fit to live in, she came with a friend to spend her first weekend there. By then Padre Pio was dead, and the two women went to visit his cell, which had just been opened to the public.

"On the way out," says Christine, "we passed a full-length portrait of the padre. I knew this painting well. It showed him looking very glum. In fact, it has since been changed for a far more agreeable one. But that day, as I looked up at his grim face, he suddenly gave us a beaming smile. He seemed absolutely delighted to see us. My friend told me if I hadn't seen it as well she would have thought she had imagined it. I was simply amazed that he was so pleased to see us."

This is a typical San Giovanni reaction. Anywhere else

FATHER JOSEPH SELDOM LEFT PADRE PIO'S SIDE AT THE
END OF HIS LIFE.

a person would have been amazed to see a portrait smile,
period.

Later that morning, as we are sitting in the office of
Father Joseph Pius in the friary, music blares all over the
piazza outside.

"Oh, dear," remarks Father Joseph, "just listen to
that!"

The "Canticle of Brother Sun" is being sung in ringing, vibrant tones, and it all sounds very festive. "They've
got 'Brother Sun' on tape," he adds. "The loudspeakers
are over there on top of the first-aid station across the
square."

Another explosion suddenly rattles the window-
panes.

"I suppose it is the young friars' joie de vivre and all
that that's responsible for all those bangs?" I ask.

"No, no, it's the old ones, actually," Father Joseph

tells me. "I just hope the picture nails are properly hammered in," he adds, as another explosion interrupts our conversation.

We are in the editorial office of the *Voice of Padre Pio*, an English-language magazine published by the friary. Father Joseph, who came over from America some years ago to become a Capuchin in the friary of Santa Maria delle Grazie, is with us. Joan, his Irish secretary, is busily tapping away at her electric typewriter. The room is spotlessly tidy, breathing order, peace, in fact, everything you would expect in a monastery except quiet.

I am here to collect information for my book, but for the moment I have no idea where to start.

My hero, Padre Pio, a very great Christian saint, is not, we are told by the church, to be described as such. But it is difficult to prevent those who knew him from doing so. A man who lived for fifty years with the wounds of the Crucifixion constantly open and bleeding, who drew hundreds and thousands of pilgrims, converted and comforted sinners and miraculously healed the sick, with hardly a murmur about his own horrific sufferings, is bound to be regarded as a saint by his spiritual children.

From the time he arrived in this lost, primitive mountain village on the east coast of southern Italy, Padre Pio rarely left the friary, where he spent his days surrounded by his brother Capuchins.

As I am rather uncertain about what a Capuchin might be, Father Joseph fills me in on the subject. The Capuchins' Rule, or fundamental code of principles, is, he says, the same as the original Franciscans', but the Order of Friars Minor Capuchin broke away from the Franciscans in 1525, during the Counter Reformation, when some members of the order decided they wanted to live in established friaries. They became known as Conventuals, from the word *convent*, still extensively used in Italy to describe monasteries or friaries of any denomination. "The heart of the rule is that we live in poverty, chastity and in obedience to the pope and his successors," Father Joseph explains. So in most respects the Capuchins are the same as the first followers of Saint Francis, the main difference being that they lead a sedentary life instead of wandering barefoot along the paths of the Italian countryside.

"There is one thing you have to be careful about with Padre Pio," says Father Joseph. "He is so tremendously great that you can't give all of him at once. Here in San Giovanni, we are used to anything happening, because there is no barrier between the supernatural and ordinary, everyday life. But when you leave this place and go back to the world, you do have to watch how you put things. Otherwise people write you off as a nut." He says this with the look of one who has suffered this fate.

"You mean not to mention too many of the extraordinary things he did?" asks Christine.

"You just have to go easy in the beginning. I'll give you an example. There was once a woman here who became aware that Padre Pio had seen Saint Francis. She grabbed him as he went past one day. 'Listen,' she said, 'next time you see Saint Francis, would you ask him to say hello to my parents in heaven?'

"'I can do that for you myself,' he answered, meaning that he could deliver her message himself, bypassing Saint Francis. You can't throw things like that at people right away. Today we are all suffering from spiritual starvation, and you shouldn't give a starving person too big a meal right away."

I agree with him in theory, but how is one to put this sensible advice into practice? Every story I have heard so far about Padre Pio is quite incredible.

"Once you know the way he lived, and some of the things he did as a matter of course," says Father Joseph, "you get a new angle on it all, and you don't wonder at it anymore."

"Is that how the people here feel about him?"

"They are never surprised at anything. They *expect* the unpredictable."

"Yes, I am beginning to get the point," I say, "but I think the only way I can tackle this is to write it as I go along and let the readers make up their own minds. They can take it or leave it. It's up to them. I am not out to convert anyone."

This little speech of mine is received without comment.

"There are more than three thousand canonized saints," Father Joseph remarks, after a pause, "but who knows their names? I can assure you there is more devotion to Padre Pio than to any other saint."

"When is he going to be canonized?"

"The Cause has been opened, but of course there is an enormous amount of material to be sorted out. Doctors will have to give evidence on the subject of all the miracles. Nobody doubts that he will be canonized in the end, but it will take time."

"Why, if they've got all the evidence?" asks Christine.

"Mostly on account of the way he was treated in his lifetime."

"How do you mean?" I ask.

"The public would be surprised at a rapid canonization after the hoops they put him through while he was alive."

"Do tell me. I know nothing of all this."

"Due to continual misunderstandings he was regarded as a charlatan, a phony, a dangerous impostor. He was spied upon. Scurrilous accusations were leveled at him. His spiritual children were called upon and questioned; he was slandered and calumniated. For years he

CHRISTINE AND MINI
ON THE BEACH
AT MATTINATA.

was confined to solitude and forbidden to say mass in public or even hear confessions. Nobody was allowed near him."

"And he submitted to this without protest?"

"Absolutely. All he ever said whenever a new restriction was imposed upon him was, 'Let God's will be done.'"

"But whoever was responsible for all this?" I ask in complete bewilderment.

"His enemies, wherever they happened to be. The forces of evil have to work through human elements, because they can't act directly."

"But they do work directly," Christine protests, "since Padre Pio was beaten up by the devil himself, in his cell."

"Yes, but that was exceptional. It only happens to the great mystical souls. The evil ones wouldn't bother to beat *me* up," says Father Joseph with a broad grin.

"And surely you wouldn't want to be!" I can't help saying. Being so new to all this, I don't fully appreciate the significance of such an event.

"We had to call the doctor in at ten o'clock that night to put stitches in the wound, which was so deep he couldn't open his eyes. Padre Pio couldn't celebrate mass the next day. A woman who came to see him three years later said to him, 'Last time I was here, padre, the devil had beaten you up.'

"'Devil!' he cried. 'They were *devils*. And they tried to scratch my eyes out.'"

As I am slowly digesting this statement, Father Joseph adds, "And the marvelous thing is, he was living in our own times; it's not as though he was a figure of medieval legend."

As Christine and I come out of the friary I feel a little bemused by the stories I have just heard; and as we step into the brilliant sunshine, the next bang makes me jump. Nobody else takes the slightest notice. People stroll in and out of church and stand around in groups, while newly arrived buses, puffing into the parking lot, disgorge large crowds of pilgrims, who make their way slowly toward the church.

It was long assumed that after Padre Pio's death, world interest in San Giovanni would decline, but, in fact, just the reverse has happened. Visitors come each year in greater numbers. Planeloads of them swoop down daily into Rome's airports and from there they proceed to Foggia. Large buses, known here as Pullmans, wheeze up the mountain road at all hours. The hotels of San Giovanni groan at the seams. Everything is packed. As Father Joseph says, the trouble with San Giovanni is that it can't keep up with its own growth and development—and with the magnetic pull of Padre Pio's personality. As the years go by, the reports of miracles and conversions continue to multiply. But then, the padre did often say that his true mission would start only after his death.

PADRE PIO AFTER BEING "BEATEN BY THE DEVILS."

THE ALTAR OF ST. FRANCIS IN SANTA MARIA DELLE GRAZIE WHERE PADRE PIO SAID MASS.

2

THE LITTLE FLOWERS
OF PADRE PIO

B Y 5:00 P.M. CHRISTINE AND I RETURN TO THE PIAZZA, waiting for the procession to begin.

More rockets go off in the friary gardens as Saint Francis is taken down from his altar in the little church. This is a special send-off for the Capuchins' patron saint, who is about to embark on his annual walkabout. As the procession forms in front of him, he stands patiently on his bed of roses and flame-colored gladioli, waiting to be picked up by the bearers who will transport him down the hill on their shoulders.

From the aisle of the original friary church, now part of the new building, Christine and I watch the Franciscan tertiaries advance in a body behind their banner. The tertiaries are a kind of civilian brigade of the third order, which was founded by Saint Francis in the thirteenth century for laymen of both sexes who live in the world but want a closer link with the religious life of the Franciscans. Behind this impressive detachment, to which most of the adult inhabitants of San Giovanni seem to belong, comes a Capuchin priest bearing aloft a golden cross. In his left hand is a microphone, into which he is singing a hymn. This is linked by a swinging cord to a loudspeaker wobbling on the shoulder of a choirboy immediately behind. Through the instrument, which faces

THE OLD SECTION OF SAN GIOVANNI ROTONDO, LITTLE
CHANGED OVER HUNDREDS OF YEARS.

backward at the crowd, comes the padre's beautiful voice, sadly distorted, sibilant and tinny. With their father guardian in the lead, the friars come next, followed by Saint Francis himself, precariously balanced on his platform. The town band falls in behind, and then, all at once, the solid mass of humanity inside the church surges implacably toward the door. Christine, who has no intention of joining the procession, stays in the depths of the little church, well away from the racket of the fireworks merrily blasting away in the square outside. But I, who wouldn't miss it for the world, am swept along by the onward rush. The squash, as we approach the door, quite literally takes my breath away. As I almost lose my balance under the charge, I begin to panic. What insane curiosity has driven me into this spot? But it is too late to back out. There is only one way out of this jam, and suddenly, with a great spurt, we are expelled through the church doors like a cork from a champagne bottle. Shaken, I step out of the crowd for a moment to get my breath back. Then, it's once more into the breach, dear friends, and forward we march behind the band.

A few parting shots are fired into the sky from the friary gardens, and the air is so still that little puffs of smoke hang above our heads like blobs of gray cotton wool. Two or three more bangs, really good loud ones this time, and we are off. Down the hill we step at a smartish pace, behind the banners and the swaying statue. The entire village is on the march: young, middling and old; men and boys; women pushing prams; toddlers sedately trotting in their polished ankle boots and white knitted stockings. Small girls prance along with wide bows sticking up from their heads like rabbits' ears, while short, plump mamas, square-shouldered and broad in the beam, follow. These, the holy women of Padre Pio, are among the most fiercely devout souls of the community. Their features, set in rugged, uncompromising lines, seem hacked out of railway ties. Their steel-gray hair is pulled back and secured to their skulls with large plastic pins. The thin, lumpy buns appear to be packed with cherry stones. Resolute and relentless, they look quite capable of trampling over anybody bold or foolish enough to stand in their way.

During Padre Pio's lifetime, these ladies gathered for mass just before 5:00 every morning on the piazza, where the rest of the faithful had already been waiting for an hour or so in the icy, nocturnal winds of the Gargano. The instant the doors opened they charged forward, scattering the waiting crowd as they surged ahead like a herd of stampeding cattle. Father Joseph tells me that the friar who opened the doors was once left suspended from the top bolt, swinging back and forth in midair, as the pack of holy women thundered past him. In their haste to get to the front, they leaped over the benches, traveling full pelt along the top of the pews on their sturdy little legs. They knocked people down and trampled over them, and their poor victims acquired a great many bumps and bruises during the charge. Each member of the holy brigade had her own self-assigned seat; and if, by any chance, some innocent visitor happened to have taken it, he or she was unceremoniously hurled into the aisle by the scruff of the neck. Meanwhile, Padre Pio patiently waited in his saintly way for the cyclone to abate, in order to start celebrating mass.

But all this was before my time, and I never saw it with my own eyes. I am simply reporting what I have been told by innumerable eyewitnesses. And now that I am plodding on after the redoubtable ladies in the procession, I have to keep nudging myself to remember that within each one of these short, determined figures marches an immortal soul in search of eternal salvation.

The *forestiere*, or "foreigners"—anyone living ten kilometers or more away—follow on behind, then come

THE MAIN PIAZZA OF SAN GIOVANNI ROTONDO.

the pilgrims from foreign parts. I guess we number a couple of thousand souls. On we go, past the postcard-and-souvenir shops and the medal-and-holy-picture emporiums, all run by people who make a living out of commercializing the holy man. There has been a lot of criticism of this in the foreign press, but Padre Pio was the first to approve of it. His children had to live, and this was, he felt, as good a way as any for them to earn their bread. And I must admit that the little shops surrounding the parking lot always look impeccably bright and festive.

Not everyone, however, is holy in this sanctified spot. Indeed, Padre Pio himself once declared that if all the devils of San Giovanni were to take flesh, they would blot out the sky, so great were their numbers. There was once an enterprising family operating as a committee to raise funds for the hospital. When a tidy sum had been collected, the committee suddenly remembered the old proverb about charity beginning at home and decided to build a house for themselves with the collection, instead of handing it over to the hospital fund. Somebody became suspicious and rang up one of the padre's female supporters, known as Little Flowers, to find out if the fund had reached its goal. The awful truth came out, and Padre Pio was duly informed. "Aha!" was all he said, and the next day the new house was found to have collapsed on its foundations.

We tramp along. The procession turns into what appears to be a side street full of rocks, ruts and potholes. But it soon becomes obvious that this has never been a street at all. New houses, products of San Giovanni's development boom, line both sides of a mountain torrent, fortunately dry at the moment. But I dread to think of it at the time of the melting of the snows. Straight ahead, Saint Francis sways giddily, as his bearers stagger along the gully. Finally we veer off to the right, and the splendid order of the procession breaks up as we all scramble up a steep, stony bank to rejoin our original road. From there, we make our way back to the hospital, to serenade its inmates. As we arrive, the more robust patients can be seen hanging over their windowsills in dressing gowns. We post ourselves beneath the windows, the band strikes up, and we burst into lusty song. Hymn follows hymn. "Brother Sun," the most haunting of them all, comes up again, and the band crashes on. Then the padre delivers a sermon in Italian, most of which, alas, is lost on me, and we set off again.

By now it is almost dark. Before long the tarred surface in front of the hospital gives way once more to a rough mountain track, and here everything goes to pieces. Half of the marchers, already ahead of the banners and the leading cross, sprint toward the church to make sure of a good seat. Infected by the general stampede, I join in the race, but by now it is almost dark, and my ankle turns over in a pothole. The strap of my sandal snaps, and I soon lose the advantage I had gained. No doubt this serves me right, and I am lucky not to have broken my ankle as well. But I eventually make it to the church, just as a shattering explosion blasts off on our right. Several rows of rockets, pegged to a number of washing lines, go off in rapid succession, sounding like a burst of machine-gun fire. Infants howl in terror, and I scamper across the square to avoid the return of the spent rockets. (A Little Flower was once set alight by one of these as it plunged back to earth.)

From the shelter of the church porch I watch the heavens, now filled with falling bursts of fire. Red, green and white stars explode at different levels, and flaming waterfalls cascade across the sky. Held aloft to get a better view, the plaster form of Saint Francis is outlined against the purple horizon, with his wire halo juddering appreciatively at the show.

The morning after, the surroundings are littered with debris from the great celebration. Christine is cleaning up her garden.

"Just look at this," she says, holding up shreds of brown paper from which dangle bits of scorched string, the whole reeking divinely of gunpowder. These remnants of homemade bombs litter the countryside. People grumble at the noise; Mini almost has a nervous breakdown and the odd Little Flower may catch fire, but I can't help rejoicing at the thought of the elderly white-haired friars dashing out of matins to wrap up their paper bombs in time to celebrate the feast day of their patron saint, as the sun comes up over the mountains in the east.

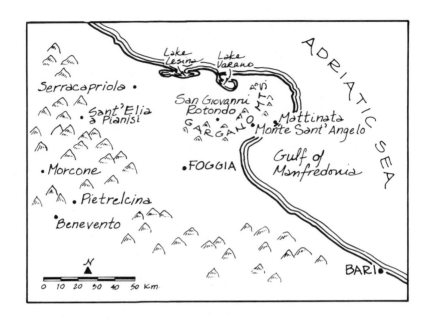

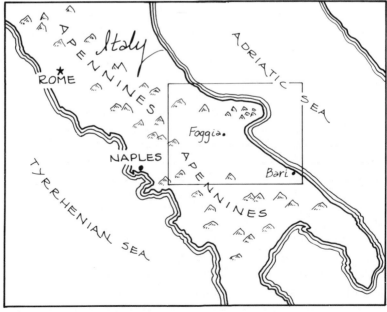

The world of Padre Pio.

· 3 ·

BOYHOOD IN PIETRELCINA

To you it is given to know the mystery of the Kingdom of God, but to the rest in parables.
LUKE 8:10

ALTHOUGH HE CAME INTO THE WORLD SEVEN CEN-
turies later, Padre Pio regarded himself as a son of
Saint Francis. Like his patron saint, he was
named Francesco, but unlike his namesake, he received
the stigmata early in his ministry on earth. (Saint Francis
received the stigmata only two years before he died.)
Born in an age of spiritual ignorance and sterility, Padre
Pio realized that he had very little time to save the world.
To bring lost souls back to God as soon as possible, he
would have to herd, hustle and browbeat them back into
the fold. "I can hit my children, I want to bring them up
fast with blows, but woe to those who lay a hand on
them," he used to say. On one occasion he told a group
of pilgrims, "Among you [humanity] I am your brother.
On the altar I am your victim. But in the confessional I
am your judge."

As a self-immolated victim for the redemption of
souls, he chose to gather in the harvest by means of the
confessional. He possessed a disconcerting knack for un-
covering sins that had not been divulged. This practice
flustered his penitents so much that they often experienced a total change of heart. Their entire lives were frequently turned upside down. With so little time in which
to salvage humanity, all he could spare them in the con-

fessional was an average of two or three minutes each. Those who came to him in an irresolute state were packed off and told to return when better disposed. Shamming or insincere penitents were thrown out almost before they entered the confessional. A young man who had come to "test" Padre Pio's powers got his ears boxed before he could even kneel down, and was chased off with furious imprecations. People often came away shaken to the roots, angry, hurt and totally confused. But after a few days of sulking they would go back to him in a different frame of mind. So these shock tactics, shattering to so many people, had a salutary effect in the end. To a woman who was desperately worried about falling into sin, he said, "As long as you are afraid to fall, you will not sin. You should be afraid when you are not afraid anymore." His tongue, sharp as a bread knife, was always at the ready. Once, when someone sympathized with him over his terrible sufferings, he snapped, "Well, a fool was needed for this."

As a victim soul, he wanted to suffer as much as anyone could while remaining alive, in order to atone for the sins of humanity. As he explained, "I love souls as much as I love God." He said he could see souls standing in front of him within their human mold even outside the confessional, most of them tarnished by sin. His greatest wish was to scrub these souls and burnish them until they shone once more like spotless reflections of the divine. It was with this end in view that he offered himself as a victim for more than fifty years of intense, unremitting suffering.

This mission of his was probably taking shape in his mind when, at the age of five, he dedicated himself to a religious way of life. He admitted to one of his spiritual daughters that he was already suffering while still in his mother's womb. And to another, who asked, "When were you consecrated to God, at your first communion, at your christening?" he answered, in dialect, "*Ne, ne, sempre, figliola, sempre*" ("Always, daughter, always").

Someone asked him once, "Padre, how much do you suffer?"

"As much as anyone who has the whole of humanity on his back," he answered.

And another time: "Everyone says, 'Poor padre, poor padre,' then they go and heap more burdens on my back."

John McCaffery, who wrote a charming and humorous book called *The Friar of San Giovanni: Tales of Padre Pio*, went to see him once at the height of an August heat wave. Padre Pio, who wore the crown of thorns as well as the stigmata and bore weals of scourging on his back, sometimes winced with pain under the scorching rays of the sun.

"Poor padre," said Mr. McCaffery. "The hot days are almost here." And it was then, adds the writer, that he received Padre Pio's first real confidence.

"No," he replied in a weary voice, "it is not so much in the daytime. You see, when the events of the day begin, one thing carries me on to the next, and so the day passes. It is the nights. If ever I allow myself to sleep, the pain of these"—holding up his wounded hands, to show the stigmata—"is multiplied beyond measure." Chances are that Padre Pio hardly ever slept; no doubt sleeplessness was part of the price he paid in the bargaining for souls that he had struck with God.

Nobody will ever know how many souls he did rescue. And his job is not yet done: "My true mission will begin after my death," he often declared.

Francesco Forgione was born on May 25, 1887, in the village of Pietrelcina, in the Samnium Hills of southern

Italy. It is a haunting, lyrical region where the bucolic life led by the people of the tiny village is little changed from medieval times.

The Samnite countryside is a pleasant succession of hills and valleys, and Pietrelcina a tightly packed cluster of houses on top of a rocky hillside. The oldest part is known euphemistically as "the castle"—which in fact it was during the Middle Ages, when the local populace took refuge within its walls from pirates' raids and constant wars between the local barons.

Francesco's birthplace, in the castle, is on the Vico Storto Valle, a passage so narrow that two people can't walk along it abreast, and a donkey's load scrapes the walls on either side. Thanks to curious inheritance laws, Grazio Forgione's "house" consisted of separate rooms at various points along the street. The main bedroom was in a building at one end and another was on the corner of the Via Santa Maria degli Angeli. Farther along the passage came the kitchen, opposite which was the donkey's cellar, where firewood was kept. Below this, a steep flight of steps cut into rock led up to a little tower room in which the young Francesco was to spend a great deal of his time studying, praying and receiving visions. Behind the kitchen was a small room used as a dining room, where his sisters slept. The cold in winter must have been horrific. Nowhere was there glass in the windows.

Francesco's parents, Grazio and Giuseppa, had bought a parcel of land an hour's walk away in a district known as Piana Romana. There, a one-room house served as the family's summer residence. The parents slept in one of the two beds, while all the children climbed into the second, to sleep as best they could. Life was hard, and so were the mattresses, stuffed and rustling with corn husks.

Throughout most of the year, when the family

stayed in the village, Grazio would set off to work at 4:00 A.M. on his donkey, pulling behind him a reluctant goat or pig at the end of a rope. By then, Giuseppa would have long since risen to make the family's bread. These loaves of Giuseppa's were a meal in themselves; crusty, heavy and packed with all the sustaining goodness of unadulterated grain. She also made goat or ewe cheese, curdling the milk over the kitchen fire and patting the curds into rounded lumps that became hard as clay when dry. She gave the whey to the children, who soaked their bread in it as a special treat. Otherwise, they lived on the fruits of the earth and of their own hard labor. Apart from bread and cheese, the family subsisted largely on olives, maize, oil and vegetables.

Altogether, the people of Pietrelcina were content in the straightforward, uncomplicated life of a small, remote village, where a sense of security grows out of age-old traditions and every day of the year comes under a pattern long laid down by the church. The saints' days, following one another around the calendar, were celebrated with fervor and hearty enjoyment.

Unlike his older brother, Michele, little Francesco cried incessantly during his first months of life. Once, his father, exasperated at being kept awake night after night, threw him roughly onto the bed, shouting, "The devil's been born in my house." In a way he was right, for as Padre Pio was to explain long afterward, he had cried out of sheer terror of the constant presence of Satan and his legions, who were constantly lurking around his cradle in the form of hideous, terrifying monsters.

At five, when he had already been having visions as far back as he could remember, he made up his mind to dedicate his life to God. When asked later why he never mentioned his visions to his mother, he said he had assumed at the time that it was a perfectly normal experience, one that everybody shared. And because of this intense spiritual life, he seldom joined in the games of other children. As he grew up, the rough manners and careless swearing and blaspheming of his young contemporaries upset him so deeply that he had to run away from them. A soul as finely and sensitively tuned as his naturally suffered from contact with the chaff of unregenerate humanity. In time, he would learn to discipline himself to the point where he could not only put up with but even love the uncouth riffraff we all are. But how we must have grated on him! More than once he remarked that he lived in the sewers of the world, and that the stench of sin was worse than that of any drain.

As a small child he was always happiest in church, staying on after the service was over and praying to the Madonna. By the age of nine he was already beginning to understand the meaning of suffering, so soon to become his chosen way of life, and he went out of his way to cultivate discomfort and penance. His mother once came upon him sleeping on the floor with a stone under his head. Another time he savagely scourged himself with a chain. When the poor, baffled woman tried to stop him, he said he was doing it for Jesus, who had received the same treatment from the Roman soldiers.

But Francesco was not only severe with himself. One Sunday, on his way home from church, he passed the house of a woman he knew. She was sitting on her doorstep, stitching a ribbon to a skirt.

"'Ndrianella, you don't work today. It's Sunday," he told her sternly.

"That's what you think, my son," she replied.

The boy dashed home and was back in a few minutes with a pair of scissors. Before the astonished woman could take evasive action, he had slashed the ribbon to pieces.

Another time, Francesco and his mother were making their way on foot to Piana Romana. "How good these look!" remarked Giuseppa, as they passed a field of broccoli. "How I'd love some!"

"That's a sin!" her son told her gruffly.

But he could also behave like a normal boy. A few days later, on the same road, he and his mother noticed that the figs were ripe on a tree they were passing. Quick as a cat, Francesco was up that tree.

"So," said his mother, "it's a sin to eat broccoli, but not figs!"

Instead of going to primary school, Francesco was sent out to the fields to look after a few sheep. But in time his father began to notice that he was not like other boys, and the thought slowly came into his head to educate Francesco, and "make a monk of him." When he was finally ready to put this idea into practice, however, Francesco was too old for the village school, and a tutor had to be found. And as he hadn't enough money to pay for the education of his precocious offspring, Grazio joined a group of men who were setting off to America "to build Brocolino" (Brooklyn).

Francesco started his studies with an unfrocked priest who was living in sin with a woman. This state of affairs affected the boy so profoundly that he was unable to work or study. He wasn't learning anything. His teacher blamed this on the fact that the boy spent hour after hour in church every day, but when his mother scolded Francesco, he blurted out, "Going to church doesn't keep me from studying. That man is a bad priest."

Giuseppa, also a sensitive soul, talked to her neighbors at Piana Romana. They had some connection with a teacher named Angelo Caccavo who ran a small private school, and they asked him to take Francesco on. But he, afraid of crossing swords with the expriest, refused. Moreover, the report on the boy was anything but encouraging. "He's an ass. Send him out to look after the sheep," said his teacher, whose conscience was no doubt disturbed by Francesco's shining innocence and uprightness.

At last, however, by a combination of pleading and threatening, Giuseppa's friends got Caccavo to take the boy on. It was in 1901. From the outset, Francesco forged ahead of his classmates. As he seldom played and was always reading, he soon acquired a wide general knowledge. He did his homework in the little tower room, where he also slept, alone and in peace.

On one occasion his schoolmates, who found him altogether much too good, wrote a love letter to one of the girls and signed it "Francesco." The girl showed it to the teacher, who was scandalized. Francesco denied having written it, but the master gave him a sound thrashing. Shaken by this development, the girl owned up, and the teacher was very penitent. All was well again, but as Padre Pio later remarked, nobody took back the beating.

All during his childhood, Padre Pio's health was precarious. Pietruccio, about whom I will write more later, tells what he calls "The Tale of the Fried Pepperone." Here it is in my rather liberal translation.

Francesco was twelve years old at the time, at home in Pietrelcina, and very ill. For forty days he had swallowed nothing but a couple of spoonfuls of milk a day. The doctor said to his mother, "I don't give him more than twenty-four hours to live. If you have a shroud, get it ready now." She began to scream. "There's nothing more I can do here," the doctor said, and hastily took his leave. The neighbors came running: "What's the matter, Giuseppa?" they wanted to know.

"My son is dying," she sobbed. By now her three daughters were also howling: "Poor boy! Poor boy!" Then in came his brother Michele.

"Francesco," he said, "would you like some milk?"

"No, no," whimpered Francesco, but Michele forced some down his throat all the same. Between sobs, Giuseppa laid out the shroud. In no way could Francesco avoid seeing the preparations for his own death.

"Michele, come here," he said in tears.

"Don't cry. Keep still. Crying will only make you worse."

"I want to go out into the fields."

"No, not now. When you're better I will take you out."

"No, I want to go now."

"But how can you manage that? How will you walk?"

"I want to go out into the fields," repeated Francesco, as firmly as his weak little voice would allow.

Just then his mother came over. "My child, keep quiet now. When you're better your mother will carry you out."

"No, no. I want to go out now, period."

Michele took his mother aside. "Listen, if he is going to die, what does it matter whether he dies here or there? Let him have his way, so he doesn't die in this terrible state of agitation."

"But how are we going to do it?"

"Leave it to me, mama." Michele took the donkey out, and climbed onto its back with Francesco in his arms. He pointed the animal in the direction of the Piana Romana, and off they set across the fields. Francesco was so weak that his head wobbled like the clapper of a bell.

The doctor, hearing of this death ride, grabbed his hat and stick and ran after them along the country road. "This is madness, pure raving lunacy!" he shouted. "Child murderer, I shall report you! Taking the boy out to his certain death . . ." And so on, until the pair were out of earshot.

Michele hurried the donkey along, and *basta*. When they reached Piana Romana, he carried his brother into the big bed and laid him on a mattress filled with corn husks. Francesco got a last dose of milk, and as the sun set, the two boys fell asleep.

The next morning, in the village, Giuseppa was getting ready to follow her sons and set off for Piana Romana. "Be brave, Giuseppa," her neighbors said. "It is now twenty-four hours and Francesco must still be living, otherwise Michele would be back."

The maize harvest was in progress at Piana Romana, and Giuseppa had fried a dish of red hot peppers, called devil's ears, for the harvesters' lunch. When she arrived, she set the dish on the dresser in the one and only room in the house, where little Francesco lay dying.

"When the delicious smell of the pepperone wafted over to me," Padre Pio told his spiritual children in the orchard all those years later, "I suddenly got an irresistible craving for them."

Giuseppa took the men's lunch out to them: boiled potatoes, the devil's ears and wine. But after one mouthful they gasped.

"No! No!" they cried. "Much too hot!"

So she brought the dish back to the house and placed it in a kind of bin on the dresser. "The men can finish them tonight," Giuseppa muttered to herself.

Next, Michele came to see how his brother was getting on. The little patient began to cry.

"Don't cry. What do you want?"

"I want the pepperone."

Michele leaped back. "Come now," he said soothingly, "have a nice spoonful of milk."

"If you give me the peppers, I will have some milk."

Michele gave him a minute scrap of the pepperone, which Francesco swallowed greedily.

"Now I want to go to sleep," he said. Michele left, but Giuseppa posted herself at the foot of the bed on a chair. Francesco began to cry.

"Why are you crying?"

"I want to go to sleep."

"Yes, go to sleep. I will keep absolutely quiet."

"No, I can't sleep because you're here."

"But I am not disturbing you. I shan't say a word."

"No, as long as you're here I can't sleep."

So the mother left and sat down outside the door.

"No, no, no," squeaked Francesco. Back she came into the room at once.

"You're behind the door, and I can't sleep. You must go away."

She felt she was going mad, but to humor him she went out behind the house, where her neighbors were shucking maize.

When Francesco heard his mother talking with the others, he eased himself up on his shoulders and very slowly put one foot out and then the other. Down he went on hands and knees and began to crawl across the room to the dresser. Grabbing it with both hands, he hauled himself to his feet and tried to lift the lid of the bin, but it was much too heavy for him. With dogged persistence, he worked away at it until he managed to get his head inside, with the lid resting on his shoulders. Then, with one grab, he snatched up a handful of devil's ears and stuffed them into his mouth.

It was like swallowing a raw flame. Another couple of handfuls and all the peppers were gone. He wiped his oily mouth with his hand and, again on all fours, set off on the return journey across the room. By the time he was back in bed, he didn't even have enough strength left to pull the covers up. He was lying there, burning like a steak on a grill, when Michele came in.

"Francesco, did you sleep?" he asked.

"No."

"Would you like a little milk?"

"Yes!"

And he swallowed eighteen spoonfuls as fast as he could.

"Here," laughed Michele, "have the bottle."

"Yes, but hold it for me."

There were only a couple of inches left at the bottom when he finished. Michele ran out of the room, bursting with the news.

"Mama, Francesco has drunk a whole bottle of milk."

"Thank God for that! Let's hope the Madonna has cured him!"

"He will surely live now. It is well over twenty-four hours."

Francesco was lying flat out, completely exhausted, when Michele came in again. "Would you like some more milk?"

"Yes." And once more he drank straight out of the bottle.

"I want to get up," Francesco said that afternoon.

"No, tomorrow," his mother said. "It's too late now, anyway."

"I want to get up, period. Now."

And the good woman had to dress him. Then she went to the bin to get the peppers out for the men's supper. As she lifted the lid, she cried out, "Not a single one left! What am I going to do? Michele, did you eat the peppers?"

"I? Certainly not!"

"Then who did? Oh, what am I to do?"

By now the workmen had gathered around.

"What's the matter? What's happened?" they asked.

"Somebody's eaten all the peppers."

"How could one person eat all those peppers? It must have been several people. A whole lot of them!"

"Francesco, did you see anyone come in?"

"I saw nobody."

"Perhaps a dog?"

"No, no dog came in. Nobody came in."

"Oh, well," said a good-natured workman. "Bread and wine will do."

The next morning, Giuseppa had to dress Francesco again and put him outside. He couldn't bear to be indoors. He even slept outside. Slowly, he began to recover. Everybody said, pointing at him, "That's the one who's risen from the dead."

When Francesco was fifteen, he told his mother he wanted to enter the religious life. For years he had noticed a dark, bearded Capuchin friar who walked about the streets of Pietrelcina from time to time begging for alms, and Francesco decided to join this order. Giuseppa consulted the parish priest, Don Pannullo, who took him on as an altar boy.

At Morcone, not far from Pietrelcina, is a Capuchin novitiate, and that is where Francesco wanted to go. For the time being, however, there were no places available. An uncle suggested the Benedictines as an alternative on the grounds that they were well-dressed, wore hats and shoes, and seemed well-fed, but these considerations were of no interest to his nephew. The uncle next proposed the Redemptorists, who also looked prosperous, and failing them, the Franciscans, who appeared sleek and comfortable—"not like those friars of Morcone, who all look consumptive." But that was precisely where Francesco insisted on going.

Jealousy and envy began to dog his footsteps again. Once more, this took the form of a letter. A poison-pen missive informed Don Pannullo that Francesco was courting one of the girls. Like the teacher before him, the shocked priest swallowed the story whole. Without checking the facts or offering Francesco any explanation, he excluded the youth from his religious obligations and for a couple of months spied on his every move. Throughout the ordeal, Francesco waited patiently for this curious trial to come to an end. Finally, the author of the letter owned up, and Francesco was reinstated. Soon after this, the provincial of the Capuchins wrote to say that there was now a vacancy.

The night before he left home, Francesco had an awesome, terrifying vision: "A majestic figure, radiant as the sun" appeared and pointed out to him a great multitude divided into two camps, one shining and beautiful, and the other hideous, dark and scowling. Between the two camps a gigantic figure was striding toward him. His guide ordered him to fight this monster, saying that he would be given help in this fearful struggle. So into battle he went, defeating the enemy and putting him and his minions to flight, while the white-robed, shining throng applauded. In a second vision, it was explained to him that the monster he had fought was the devil and that he would have the formidable task of waging war against the same enemy for the rest of his life. These visions bolstered his resolution, giving him the courage to leave his mother, his home and the world behind.

· 4 ·

FRA PIO

O N JANUARY 3, 1903, FRANCESCO PRESENTED HIM-
self at the monastery of Morcone. Like all postulants he had to assume a new identity, and he
received the name Pio, Italian for "Pius," in honor of
Saint Pius V, patron saint of Pietrelcina. Henceforth, for
the next seven years and more, he would be called
Brother Pius—Fra Pio.

The novitiate is a year-long succession of trials intended to put off weak souls. The program worked out
for this purpose is formidable. What is amazing is that
anybody should survive it and still want to carry on in,
so to speak, the same line of business. Only with powerful supernatural help is this possible, and novices unable
to plug into the heart of this spiritual reservoir drop away
like dead leaves in autumn. By the end of the novitiate
year only a handful of the original postulants are left
standing and battling. Once you survive that year, you
can put up with anything. No hardship will ever again
dismay you.

The life of a novice at Morcone was unbelievably
rigorous. The region of Apulia in southeastern Italy,
swept all winter by winds from the Russian Urals, is hideously cold. The monastery was of course unheated. The
novices were allowed one woolen undershirt beneath

their habits, and their feet went virtually bare in drafty sandals. Food was sparse and deliberately made as unpalatable as possible. The boys, most of them peasants from surrounding farms and villages, were used to eating their fill of simple but wholesome fare at home. At fifteen, moreover, a boy is still growing and needs plenty of solid nourishment, but this they certainly did not get in the friary. Their meager diet was reduced still further by endless restrictions. Every Friday, fasting was of course compulsory. Then came long weeks of abstinence to honor the Blessed Virgin, lasting from June 30 until August 14. Preparation for Christmas began on November 2 and lasted until December 25; then only a few weeks later came Lent. Altogether, that year must have seemed like one long, very lean run to the novices.

Even when these famished teenagers were not obliged to fast, eating was hardly a pleasure. On the feast days of the Madonna and the saints of the order, they had to eat on their knees—not picnic fashion, but kneeling on the floor. By then, I imagine, they would gladly have eaten hanging upside down if necessary. On ordinary days, to make sure they didn't commit the sin of greed, one of them had to ask the master of novices to bless them. They were lucky if he did, for as often as not he pretended not to hear, with the result that they had to stay on their knees until he chose to give them his blessing. Sometimes he simply left them there and went off to attend to other business. On one occasion, a youth who was driven to the end of his patience remarked that in Naples you had to pay to see a madman, whereas in the novitiate you could see one every day of the year free of charge. He had to scourge himself for that wisecrack, and afterward he disappeared from the scene altogether.

But in spite of all these rigors and austerities, there were always more applications from would-be postulants than there were vacancies. Besides, mortification of the flesh brought rewards in the shape of divine graces descending on these aspiring young souls, which glowed with ever-increasing ardor. But it was not only the flesh that had to be mortified. The novice's ego, too, was slowly but inexorably eroded until finally it was extinguished altogether.

A novice training for the priesthood was—and is—obliged absolutely to obey his master in all things. Throughout his life Padre Pio would unfailingly observe this rule, and when his friends fumed and raged at the humiliating and insulting restrictions that were placed on him, he would reply, "The more ridiculous the order, the more willingly I obey it."

Each novice had a tiny cell containing a bed, a chair, a table and a washstand holding a jug of cold water. The bedding was no more than a sack filled with corn husks lying on top of a board. Fra Pio slept on this in his clothes after prayers and a meticulous examination of conscience. He lay on his back, not to encourage sleep but to defend himself against the devil's assaults, with sensuality the number-one temptation. With his arms crossed over his chest, a large crucifix threaded through his belt and not enough blankets to keep the cold out, there was a chance that the flesh might be sufficiently mortified to resist such temptation. In case this wasn't enough, the master of novices, who took no chances, wakened his charges at midnight to go sing lauds and matins in the choir. Shivering along the corridors in their bare feet, their teeth chattering with cold, and yawning with drowsiness, the friarlings staggered on to praise the Lord and thank Him for all His mercies. It was not always easy to go back to sleep after that. Some had just managed to drop off when they were roused again at five for prayer and meditation.

Mass was at eight, then breakfast, after which came a study of the rules. At eleven the novices did the housework, and at noon they went in to lunch. This was followed by half an hour in the garden, reciting prayers. Study went on until five, and then came more meditation and the rosary. At eight supper was served, after which half an hour's recreation wound up the day before bed at nine.

Ever since I first met them, I regarded the Capuchin friars at San Giovanni with warm affection. But now that I know this schedule, and what they went through at the age of fifteen, my feelings also include deepest awe and respect.

But I haven't finished yet. Punishment for any infringement of the rule was severe. A wooden collar was placed around the neck of the poor wretch, or a black bandage tied over his eyes. Another penance was to eat off the floor in full view of the other novices.

Then there was the discipline. This could be ordered at any time of the day and had to be carried out at once. If it struck in the middle of a meal the victim had to retire behind the door to carry out the sentence. If during recreation, his colleagues formed a ring around him while he scourged his bare flesh with a chain loaded with bits of lead. These barbaric customs, it must be remembered, were taken on by the boys of their own free will. Nobody ever forced anyone into a novitiate. In fact, it was not easy to stay there either. Four times a year, a vote was taken among friars and novices, and those who were unpopular, or not deemed worthy of the life, were blackballed, or rather chickpeaed. (Each novice was handed a broad bean, which meant yes, he could stay, or a chickpea, which signaled instant dismissal.)

The novices who remained had to undergo discipline three times a week as a matter of routine. This took place in the choir after supper. Each boy was handed a scourge, the lights were blown out, and without further ado they had to begin pulling their habits up to their shoulders and whipping their own bare flesh with the lead-loaded chain. There was always blood on the floor after these religious exercises. The object of all this was to make the flesh obedient to the spirit, since everybody knows about the one being willing and the other weak. The boys, while they scourged themselves to the quick, were supposed to meditate at the same time—if they were able—on the Passion of Our Lord, and force themselves to take part in His sufferings.

The master watched over them day and night, walking into their cells whenever he felt like it without knocking and often imposing the discipline, not necessarily as a punishment but simply to instill the habit of obedience.

So much for the flesh. For the spirit, there was frequent confession. And four times a year an "extraordinary confessor" came to the monastery to hear the confessions of every one of the postulants.

In his book *Padre Pio, Childhood and Adolescence,* Gherardo Leone writes that Fra Pio "gave the whole of himself to this building of character. He dedicated all his energy to it, with the perseverance he showed in everything . . . complete renunciation of his own will; scorn of himself; detachment from inclinations and affections incompatible with his religious state; increasing mortification of the senses; self-control at every circumstance; patience, constancy, purity of the senses and the heart." Altogether, a walking miracle. And of course, at the end of the year, he came out at the top in everything.

At the end of this grueling period Fra Pio was sent to other friaries in the monastic province of Foggia to continue his studies. He spent most of this time at Sant' Elia a Pianisi, where he read philosophy. In 1907 he took his final vows of poverty, chastity and obedience in the Capuchin order and from then on was a full-blown friar.

In the opening years of the century, when Fra Pio was studying for the priesthood, the winter cold, his wretched diet, and the fasts and penances he inflicted upon himself told heavily on his health. Several times, raging fevers, chest pains and breathing difficulties forced him to quit the monastery and return home for a time. These interruptions of his studies worried him, and he despaired at the thought of his ordination being put off indefinitely. Yet there could be no doubt that the air of Pietrelcina improved his condition. Back in his old tower room he could study and pray in peace, as well as receive frequent visits from Jesus and the Madonna. When the summer came and his family moved to Piana Romana, he built himself a hut of twigs and foliage. During this period his abiding fear was that he would never become a priest. And he was not the only one who was worried. The provincial of the Capuchin order, who thoroughly disapproved of the situation, wanted Fra Pio back in the fold as soon as possible.

At last, his home studies were recognized as valid, and the date of his ordination was fixed. The ceremony took place in Benevento Cathedral on August 10, 1910, and the new priest celebrated his first mass the following Sunday in the parish church of Pietrelcina. It was then that he offered himself formally as a victim for the salvation of sinners and the freeing of souls in purgatory. This, he now knew for certain, was to be his mission on earth. As he was still too frail to go back to community life, he wrote long and frequent letters to his spiritual director, Padre Benedetto. For weeks and months on end he constantly meditated on the sufferings of Christ. As a result, he himself endured frightful torments, both mental and physical.

"This is a suffering which is good for me," he wrote Padre Benedetto, going on to explain that it made it possible for him to work his way through to a kind of "peace and tranquility"—the best he could hope for at the time. And in this frame of mind he continued for the next six years until he finally arrived in the remote region of the Gargano Mountains, which would be his home until the end of his life.

· 5 ·

THE GARGANO

NOBODY OUTSIDE ITALY SEEMS TO HAVE HEARD OF the Gargano. "You know," I try to explain, "the bit that sticks out into the Adriatic."
"Oh, you mean the heel of the boot?"
"No, higher up. It's usually called the spur."

As the last remaining chunk of the Land of Adria, which used to join the Dinaric Alps to Italy, the Gargano is all that is left of an ancient land bridge that sank beneath the sea in prehistoric times; all, that is, except for the Tremiti Islands and the nine hundred ninety-nine islands of Dalmatia. Rising to about three thousand feet, the Gargano juts out sixty-five miles into the sea. Formed for the most part of chalk sprinkled with deposits of karst, the peninsula is riddled with caves and crisscrossed with underground streams, which crash and tumble deep inside the heart of the mountain on their way to the sea. The surface, dry and bleak and strewn with white stones, looks like the arid slopes of the Holy Land around Jerusalem. Shepherds still dress as their ancestors did; and when you see one standing on a height surrounded by his flock, you have no trouble at all imagining yourself back in biblical times.

This wild, desolate landscape has a haunting and bewitching quality that can get under the skin. Covered

GOATS AND SHEEP GRAZING ON THE DESOLATE GARGANO
LANDSCAPE.

ARRIVING AT MONTE SANT' ANGELO, HIGHEST PEAK OF
THE GARGANO, FROM SAN GIOVANNI.

with snow in winter, the slopes are swept by icy blasts howling across the Adriatic from the frozen wastes of the Urals. In summer, the dried-out vegetation crackles in the heat to the screech of innumerable insects. Even though, at first sight, the terrain looks as dead as the moon, life, in fact, crawls, hops and flutters over every inch of it. Cicadas cluster in their millions in the thorny scrub. Huge lizards abound, and horned vipers take their ease, curled up on hot stones in the sun. Birds of every kind raise their young in the spiny gorse and thorn bushes, and high above all of this intense, throbbing life cruise the hawks, constantly stooping to kill, kill, kill.

The mountains of the Gargano have been inhabited since earliest times. The original natives, known as the Daunians, flourished in Paleolithic days and were presumably wiped out by invaders. Within historical time there came in succession Greeks, Romans, Byzantines, Arabs, Normans, Swabians and Aragonese, all slaughtering and burning. But in spite of the wholesale destruction that accompanied each invasion, traces of these different cultures and races can still be found throughout the peninsula.

It is now October. Early one morning, as the rising sun shimmers through a fragile butter-muslin mist, Christine announces that we are off to Monte Sant' Angelo, the highest peak of the Gargano. She wraps up a picnic in a multitude of little plastic bags. Mini, hysterical with excitement, leaps into the driver's seat, and off we set into the biblical landscape of the eastern peninsula. Great stretches of black, scorched earth spread out on either side. Here and there in these fields of burnt stubble are scattered flocks of incredibly thin sheep. Whatever can they find to eat in those calcinated deserts?

The mountain town of Sant' Angelo is dedicated to the cult of Saint Michael, Prince of Heaven, who led the seraphic host against the rebellious Lucifer and pitched

AN OLIVE GROVE OF THE GARGANO.

him out of Paradise. In Sant' Angelo, Saint Michael established his earthly headquarters, for which he could
hardly have found a wilder, more rugged and formidable
approach. He appeared in person in a cave deep underground on four different occasions. When the town of
Sant' Angelo later sprang up around this grotto, a great
basilica was built above it. Within its depths Saint Michael appeared for the first time in A.D. 490, when the

Houses tightly clustered atop a hill in Monte Sant' Angelo.

lord of Monte Gargano was searching for a lost bull. Climbing among the rocks, the chief finally ran the animal to earth at the entrance of the great cavern, where the bull was on its knees in what appeared to be a trance. Puzzled, the tribal chief shot an arrow at it, but to his amazement the arrow turned in midair and came back to strike him instead. When he reported this astonishing event to the bishop, a three-day fast was immediately proclaimed. At the end of this the Prince of Heaven appeared, saying, "I am the Archangel Michael and am always in the presence of God. The cave is sacred to me and is of my own choosing. There is to be no more shedding of bull's blood in this place. Where the rocks open wide, the sins of man may be pardoned. That which is asked here in prayer will be granted. Therefore, go up to the mountain and dedicate the grotto to the cult of Christianity." (At that time, pagans still thrived and prospered there.)

A few years later, the wild hordes of the local chieftain, Odoacre, attacked the Christian settlement of Siponto on the coast, not far from the hideous present-day industrial town of Manfredonia. The Christians, besieged by the savage enemy, were about to surrender when the bishop, with great presence of mind, asked Odoacre for a three-day truce. A master of strategy, the bishop knew that nothing should be done in a hurry. After the truce came another three-day fast, at the end of which the archangel appeared once more. He promised to help the Christians if they attacked the pagan hordes. So, led by the bishop, out they rushed from the town walls, full of courage and determination. Coming to their help, a heavenly host rained upon their enemy a shower of sand and hail. At this point, the forces of Odoacre took to their heels.

There followed a procession of thanksgiving on the mountain. But still the bishop, in his humility, was reluctant to enter the holy cave. A year later, still worried about his unworthiness, he asked the pope's advice on the matter. His Holiness declared that he must obey the archangel's orders. After another three days' fast to clear the spirit, off he set with a cohort of neighboring bishops.

When they arrived on the spot, the Prince of Heaven appeared once more. "Go inside," he urged. "You will

THE TOWER OF ST. MICHAEL'S BASILICA.

see how I myself have consecrated the place." They went in and there found an altar covered with a red cloth, on which stood a crystal crucifix. Impressed into the rock they saw the form of an infant footprint.

The angel's last appearance was in 1656, at the height of a plague epidemic. After ordering prayers and fasting, the bishop of the time invoked the Prince of Heaven. This time he came, saying, "I am the Archangel

AN UNDERGROUND PASSAGEWAY IN MONTE SANT' ANGELO.

Michael. Anyone who uses the stones of this grotto will be cured of the plague." He then instructed the people to bless the stones and carve his name upon them with a cross. According to local lore, as they obeyed, they were cured at once.

The Prince of Heaven, who had conquered Lucifer and cast him into hell, must have seemed the greatest hero of all time to Padre Pio, whose own life was so constantly plagued by demons. But in spite of his special devotion, there is no record that Padre Pio chose San Giovanni because of its nearness to the holy mountain, or that he even visited the grotto.

In any event, in 1916 his spiritual director, who had been trying for some time to extract the young priest from Pietrelcina and send him back to community life, managed to persuade him to go to Foggia, where one of his spiritual daughters lay dying. More than anything, she wanted to see Padre Pio. And so he went, giving her the comfort and assistance she needed before her long journey into eternity.

Summers in Italy are notoriously hot and stifling, but this was a particularly steaming and sultry one. With his asthma and his unreliable bronchial tubes, Padre Pio had difficulty breathing. The long hot nights left him panting and unable to sleep. Seeing him in this pitiful state, the father guardian of Our Lady of Grace took him off to the Gargano, where you can usually rely on refreshing breezes blowing around the mountain slopes. In July, they set off for San Giovanni Rotondo.

Except for several brief but disastrous spells in the army, Padre Pio was to stay there for the rest of his life.

PADRE PIO SOON AFTER RECEIVING THE STIGMATA.

· 6 ·

THE STIGMATA—
AND AFTER

ONE DAY, AS FATHER JOSEPH AND I ARE IN THE
sacristy, idly chatting, he suddenly says out of
the blue: "I don't know why it is, but all the
books get the facts wrong about the stigmata."

"I suppose all kinds of rumors have been going
around since Padre Pio's death?"

"Correct."

"Well, won't you tell me the true facts?"

"To begin with, Padre Pio was *not* found lying in a
pool of blood in a dead faint at the foot of the crucifix, in
the choir of the old church."

"How did it happen, then?"

"For nine whole days nobody knew anything about
it. Then, when the friar who was changing the linen on
his bed found blood on the sheets, he told the father
guardian, and Padre Pio had to confess to exactly what
had happened," continues Father Joseph.

It was on a hot day in early August 1918, as he was
hearing a boy's confession, that he received the wound in
his side.

It is not within my power to describe or even give an
inkling of this mystical happening. All I can do is to
quote Padre Pio's own words (in translation) on the
event, written to his spiritual director:

I was suddenly filled with great terror at the sight of a heavenly person who presented himself to my mental gaze. He held in his hand a kind of weapon, like a very long, sharp-pointed blade, which seemed to emit fire. At the very instant in which I saw all this, that person hurled the weapon into my soul with all his might. I cried out with difficulty and thought I was dying. I asked the boy to leave because I felt ill and no longer had the strength to continue. This agony lasted uninterruptedly until the morning of the 7th. I cannot tell you how much I suffered during this period of anguish. Even my entrails were torn and ruptured by that weapon and nothing was spared. From that day on I have been mortally wounded. I feel in the depths of my soul a wound that is always open and causes me continual agony.

After this, he was plunged into the "dark night of the soul" for several weeks. God seemed to have abandoned him. He wandered about the corridors of the friary weeping and moaning: "Where is Jesus? Why has He left me?" Then on September 20, the stigmata appeared on his hands and feet. He had been sitting in the choir making his thanksgiving after mass when a "great light" suddenly shone before him, and in it appeared the figure of the wounded Christ. It was, he said later, the crucifix before which he was praying that was transformed into a celestial being emitting "beams of light and shafts of flame." It was these flames which pierced his hands and feet. Once more I leave it to the padre's own pen to describe what happened next:

I was suddenly filled with great peace and abandonment which effaced everything else and caused a lull in the turmoil. All this happened in a flash.

PADRE PIO RECEIVED THE STIGMATA WHILE PRAYING BEFORE
THIS CRUCIFIX.

Meanwhile I saw before me a mysterious person, similar to the one I had seen on the evening of August 5th. But this time, his hands and feet and side were dripping blood. The sight frightened me, and what I felt at that moment cannot be described. I thought I should die, and indeed I should have died if the Lord had not intervened and strengthened my heart, which was about to burst out of my chest.

The vision disappeared and I became aware that my own hands and feet and side were dripping blood. Imagine the agony I experienced and continue to experience almost every day. The heart wound bleeds continually, especially from Thursday evening until Saturday. Dear Father, I am dying of pain because of the wound and the resulting embarrassment. I am afraid I shall bleed to death if the Lord does not hear my heartfelt supplication to relieve me of this condition. . . . I will raise my voice and not stop imploring Him.

But the Lord did not hear his plea—far from disappearing, Padre Pio's wounds became more pronounced. The father guardian made the padre's spiritual daughters promise to keep quiet about the stigmata, but some couldn't resist telling their families and friends. Soon, all of San Giovanni Rotondo was in on the secret. And after the war ended, in November, the news began to reach the great world outside. Early in 1919, the first pilgrims appeared at the friary of Santa Maria delle Grazie. Before long their numbers swelled to dozens, then hundreds.

As there was no accommodation for visitors in San Giovanni or anywhere near the friary, tents began to appear on the stony fields all around. A shifting, motley population settled down to this nomadic way of life under canvas, and there was a good deal of bustling and cheerful coming and going, shouts and clatter and never-ending hubbub and commotion. There were, of course, no sanitary facilities, and the civil authorities became increasingly perturbed.

Meanwhile, the church administration was disturbed by this show of veneration for a simple country priest. From Rome, the head of the Capuchin order and highly placed prelates in the Vatican sent eminent physicians to examine Padre Pio's stigmata. Although these doctors did not agree as to the precise nature of the wounds, none doubted their authenticity. In 1921 Pope Benedict XV called the padre "an extraordinary man, the like of whom God sends to earth from time to time for the purpose of converting men." The following year, however, Pope Benedict died, and his successor, Pius XI, was less ready to accept supernatural explanations for such events as the appearance of the stigmata. He ordered a thorough investigation of the affair. Padre Pio was, in effect, placed under arrest. From then on, he could only offer mass at a different and unannounced hour each day and was forbidden to show the stigmata or speak of them, bless crowds or answer letters from his spiritual children too ill to visit him, not even from Padre Benedetto, who had helped him so much.

So began, for Padre Pio, a period of harassment by the Vatican that would last for more than a decade. He regarded these trials as part of his calvary and would never allow anybody to take up the cudgels on his behalf. Putting up with injustices was essential to the vow of obedience he had undertaken.

During this period, Lucia Fiorentino, one of Padre Pio's followers, had a vision of an enormous tree whose shade covered the whole world. All who took shelter under its branches, Jesus had told her, would be saved, and all who mocked it punished. Early in 1923, Lucia declared: "Now I understand that this tree is Padre Pio, who, coming from afar, has taken root in the monastery according to the will of God." She foresaw that he was going to suffer further persecution, and she offered her life to the Lord in exchange for his liberation.

These further persecutions were not long in coming. In June, the padre was ordered to stop celebrating mass in public, whereupon the whole village, with the mayor in the lead, marched on the friary and forced the father guardian to rescind the order. Suspecting that the ecclesiastical authorities were hoping to defuse the Padre Pio problem by moving him elsewhere, the townspeople set up a day-and-night guard around the friary. When orders to transfer the padre to Ancona arrived from Capuchin headquarters in August, the discovery that this could only be done at the cost of bloodshed made the authorities think better of it. In the end, he was allowed to stay on at the friary.

For the next eight years, Padre Pio carried on his mission in the teeth of new restrictions further limiting his contacts with the people. Because of his stigmata, the continuing reports of miracles he had wrought and the fanatical devotion of his followers, he remained, in the eyes of many churchmen, a controversial and suspect figure. Then, in April of 1931, a new crisis boiled up. Convinced that the Vatican was plotting anew to transfer Padre Pio elsewhere, the people of San Giovanni again posted an armed guard around the friary, a force that would remain in place for two years and more.

During this period that he called his "imprisonment," Padre Pio lived completely cut off from the world. Although they could neither see him nor hear him, the faithful continued to pour into San Giovanni to pray for his release. And his supporters bombarded the Vatican with pleas on his behalf.

At last, Lucia Fiorentino's sacrificial offer was accepted, and God took her life in exchange for Padre Pio's freedom. On July 14, 1933, Pope Pius reversed his ban, allowing the padre once again to celebrate mass in public and hear the confessions of his fellow friars. "I have not been badly disposed towards Padre Pio," the pope told an archbishop, "but I have been badly informed about him." In time, the Vatican lifted other restrictions on the padre. On March 25, 1934, he was once more permitted to hear the confessions of men, and on May 12 those of women.

By 1935 the crowds were beginning to come back to San Giovanni, and in August Padre Pio was getting ready to celebrate the twenty-fifth anniversary of his first mass, in the open air on the piazza, before thousands of people. It was to be a great paean of love and thanksgiving, in which the faithful from far and near would take part in a High Mass with a liturgical choir. The padre's spiritual sons brought him marvelous vestments for the occasion. A feeling of rejoicing and festivity was in the air. The village was in a state of joyful expectation.

Then, at the last minute, came another crack of the whip. There was to be no High Mass after all, only a simple service with three priests, and *no singing*—in fact, a subdued, early-morning Low Mass, as usual. But it was a joyful and glorious day nonetheless.

· 7 ·

THE CASA

WHEN HE CAME TO SAN GIOVANNI IN 1916, young Padre Pio found an undeveloped town with no plumbing and no electricity, its inhabitants living in miserable stone hovels. Right away he began to build kindergartens, which gradually turned into orphanages. These he staffed with nuns (and they are still functioning today).

There was still no decent road out of San Giovanni, and in winter the torrents rushing down the rocky slopes always washed away the tracks of the carts. Even in good weather it took twelve hours to get to Foggia by horse or bullock power, and trips to the hospital there too often ended tragically. But even worse than this was the appalling poverty of the region. Before the days of national health, their near-total destitution prevented the people from seeking medical aid, even in the exceptional circumstances when it was available. This pathetic state of affairs was a gnawing worry to Padre Pio, for the little Saint Francis hospital he had founded in 1925 to provide free medical care could serve only a tiny fraction of the community's health needs. Many of the pilgrims, moreover, drawn to San Giovanni by the hope of being miraculously cured of their ills, urgently required medical attention.

What was he to do? The solution, the padre saw, would be to build a big, modern hospital right in the Gargano. And it so happened that during the middle years of the 1930s there came to San Giovanni, separately, three medical men who would help him realize this immensely ambitious project. They were Dr. Guglielmo Sanguinetti of Florence; Dr. Mario Sanvico, a veterinarian from Perugia; and Dr. Carlo Kisvarday, a pharmacist from Yugoslavia.

Dr. Sanguinetti was a bluff, jolly man with an enormous capacity for work. But much to the grief of his pious wife he had always been very anticlerical. One year, as their wedding anniversary approached, he asked her what she wanted for a present.

"A visit to San Giovanni Rotondo," was her hopeful reply.

"Oh, no," said her husband. "That's not fair. Ask me for anything, but not that."

In the end, however, kind man that he was, he said, "Very well, if that's what you really want, we will go." With these words he sealed his destiny. As soon as he looked into the eyes of Padre Pio he "saw something there he had never seen before in his life. He gave in without a struggle."

"You, doctor, are the man who will come here and build my hospital," the padre told him.

"I? But I am neither an architect nor an engineer," Sanguinetti protested, "simply a doctor of medicine. Besides, I could never afford to give up my practice and come here to live on faith."

"God will provide," said Padre Pio. And he urged the doctor to go home, settle his affairs, and come back.

Within a couple of weeks of returning to Florence, Dr. Sanguinetti won a large sum of money in the national lottery, a development he saw as Providence working in accordance with Padre Pio's plans. With a part of his

DR. GUGLIELMO SANGUINETTI.

winnings, he bought a farm, which he let out to provide himself with an income. The rest was spent building a house on the first available plot of land in San Giovanni. As nobody told him he was planting his house in one of the worst flood areas of town, the doctor often had to set off to work up to his ankles in water.

Padre Pio seems to have used a much less direct approach with Dr. Sanvico. According to an account by one of his spiritual sons, Pietruccio, of a conversation between the two, the padre let his visitor think the hospital was his, the doctor's, idea.

"Padre," said the doctor, "why don't you do something for those poor people?"

"My son, again and again something of this sort comes into my mind. It gives me no peace. See how terribly poor they all are and how isolated we are in this abandoned district."

"Padre," said the doctor, "we will build them a hospital."

"That is exactly what I've been wanting to do for a long time. But how are we going to do it?"

"Your spiritual sons will help you. We are at your service."

"Fine. But how will we set about it?"

"The Lord will guide our hands."

With Dr. Kisvarday, finally, Padre Pio was decidedly blunt: "Build yourself a house here," he commanded. Obediently, the new recruit bought a piece of land and built his house—on high ground, safe from the winter floods.

In August 1938, an earthquake struck San Giovanni Rotondo, with tremors that went on for a whole month afterward. It severely damaged the friary, forcing Padre Pio and the other friars to sleep in an ambulance in the friary gardens. It also demolished the little Saint Francis hospital. But the padre, with plans for a big hospital taking shape in his mind, wasn't interested in rebuilding it.

Unaware of this, however, an old woman he knew approached him one day and begged him to accept, as her contribution to rebuilding the Saint Francis hospital, a five-lire coin, worth next to nothing. He waved her away.

"No, my daughter," he said kindly, "you need this money yourself. I know how things are with you."

"But, padre, I can manage if I stop being so extravagant. I don't need to buy matches anymore. My neighbors say I can get a light from their fire."

"The Lord doesn't demand such sacrifices from his children."

"I know it isn't much. Perhaps it's not enough. . . ."

Padre Pio, who by now must have had a lump in his throat, accepted the coin, and after that he always kept it in his pocket. "See this," he would say to visitors, producing it, and then he would tell the story.

The last time he produced the coin was on an evening in January 1940, when Sanguinetti, Sanvico and Kisvarday were with him in his cell. "I want to make this first donation to the House for the Relief of Suffering," he told them, before announcing his full plans for the hospital. Padre Pio always referred to the hospital as the House for the Relief of Suffering. Its official name is the Casa Sollievo della Sofferenza, or more commonly, the Casa.

All three doctors were enthusiastic about the project, but they warned him that with Europe at war, the time was hardly propitious for raising funds. Five months later, Italy entered the war on the side of Nazi Germany. Even as fighting raged on the very soil of Italy, however, Padre Pio never missed an opportunity to collect contributions for his cherished hospital. When peace was restored at last, he launched a nationwide appeal. Donations poured in, all but a handful in very modest amounts.

Meanwhile, in addition to his three doctors, Padre Pio acquired the services of an architectural genius, Don Angelo Lupi. The site the padre had picked, on land one of his spiritual daughters had donated, was as barren as the moon.

"Padre, this is a graveyard, but we will put it here all the same," said Lupi, morosely regarding the stretch of rock-strewn mountainside.

At last, in May 1947, there was enough cash on hand to begin construction. Dr. Sanguinetti made himself over into a construction expert. Starting before dawn, he could be seen driving trucks through the mud, the snow, the floods. He supervised gangs of laborers, selected building materials and taught himself a host of new skills. By the time the hospital was finished, there was nothing a builder could do that he couldn't.

As soon as the Casa began to take shape, Dr. Kisvarday became its treasurer. Padre Pio took enormous pleasure in watching the building's progress. Every day he would peer out at it from the little choir window. "Look at these workmen," he would say happily. "They really are getting on with it."

Whenever people praised him for the achievement, he would say, "You've done it yourselves. You gave the money and that's what is making the building go up."

"Padre, we give very little. If it wasn't for you, where would we be?"

"Ah, bah, let us give the honor to God. It was the Lord who made use of this stupid Padre Pio, for His own ends."

After only a few months, however, the money ran out and construction came to a halt. The project was in trouble, but then help came from an unexpected source. In the summer of 1948, Barbara Ward, a British writer on economics and international politics, came to Italy to look into the operation there of the United Nations Relief and Rehabilitation Administration, or UNRRA. From Rome, her friends the Marquis and Marchioness Patrizzi took her to San Giovanni Rotondo, where they stayed with the Sanguinettis. Convinced that the padre's hospital would fill a real and pressing need, Miss Ward wrote her fiancé, Comdr. Robert Jackson of UNRRA, about the matter, and as a result that big international organization made a grant of $325,000 toward the construction of the Casa.

With the hospital almost finished, Dr. Sanguinetti, as resourceful as ever, turned to other projects. His next venture was to set up a farm from which to provide patients with fresh dairy and vegetable produce. That done, he decided to transform the barren slopes of Monte Calvo behind the friary into a flourishing woodland. When the Department of Agriculture declared this to be impossible, Sanguinetti dynamited the rock, had thousands of tons of soil hauled up the slopes on muleback and proceeded to plant an entire forest. The ten thousand saplings he planted have since seeded a whole generation of new ones. The undergrowth is full of shrubs and flowering bushes, and the ground is covered with violets and wild cyclamen; birds build their nests in the foliage, butterflies flit among the flowers and squirrels race about in the trees. This virgin paradise, which extends over several acres of a mountain that can no longer properly be called Monte Calvo ("Bald Mountain") is the creation of the indefatigable Dr. Sanguinetti.

But even as he rejoiced to see these transformations taking place all around him, Padre Pio was saddened by premonitions of impending loss. One day in the early 1950s, when the hospital directors all happened to be assembled together, he said with a sigh, "Two of us will not see the completion of this work." More than that he would not say. And on an evening in early September 1954, Dr. Sanguinetti brought him a present from the hospital farm in the form of a beautiful, luscious peach.

A few days later, Padre Pio asked, "Who will bring me a peach tomorrow?"

"I will," said Sanguinetti. The padre shook his head. "Ah, who will bring me a peach tomorrow?" he repeated, as if he hadn't heard the doctor's offer. And nobody did, because Sanguinetti was dead the following day, the victim of a heart attack. (Dr. Sanvico would be the next to go, dying of cancer seven months later.)

The House for the Relief of Suffering was at last opened officially on the padre's feast day, May 5, 1956.

Sanguinetti's death, in particular, was a terrible blow to Padre Pio. "Ah," he said sadly, "one after the other, the Lord calls them home."

Again his words were prophetic, for in the summer of 1960 Dr. Kisvarday, the sole survivor among the original hospital directors, breathed his last.

That year, for the first time since the 1930s, Padre Pio again had to endure restrictions and humiliation at the hands of church authorities. From Rome came an "apostolic visitation" to investigate him and his ministry, particularly regarding the Casa. This in turn led to the questioning of local people, orders to report directly to the Vatican and terrible insinuations about the padre's conduct. Once more he was locked up and forbidden to see anyone. This went on until 1963, when the new superior released him from all restrictions. Once more he was surrounded by his beloved, sinful souls.

By 1968, the padre's health was failing. Frequently ill, he remained in his cell and from there talked through a microphone to the crowds clustering beneath his window. When he felt a little better, he would go down to the terrace with the help of a few of the friars. With his rosary in his fingers, he would sit there absorbed in prayer and meditation.

One evening in mid-September he stumbled as he was leaving the altar, having said his last mass. Father Joseph caught him just in time. Then, in the corridor, on his way to the elevator, Padre Pio collapsed. Within a few hours he was dead. One of the doctors present later said it was the sweetest and most peaceful death he had ever witnessed.

As the friars stood in silent prayer around him, did they recall Padre Pio's saying he would be able to do more for humanity after his death than he had in life?

PADRE PIO AMONG HIS SPIRITUAL SONS, WITH FATHER
JOSEPH BEHIND HIM AND FATHER ALESSIO AT HIS LEFT.

· 8 ·

THE STORY OF
FATHER JOSEPH

CHRISTINE AND I HAVE BEEN INVITED TO TEA AT THE friary. We follow Father Joseph, who leads us into one of the innumerable rooms with which the seventeenth-century building is honeycombed. These are small, bare and whitewashed, typical convent rooms. If there isn't any linoleum on the floor, then there ought to be.

On a small table surrounded by four hard chairs is a tray, beautifully laid and ready for tea. The crockery is buttercup-yellow earthenware, and there are handcarved little wooden spoons from Monte Sant' Angelo. Father Joseph pours and hands around dainty biscuits. Today, all is quiet: no fireworks, no rockets, no bangs.

"Have you heard the Roversi story?" asks our host. "No? Well, you know Signora Roversi who runs Abresch, the picture-and-souvenir shop?"

We nod.

"Well, when her daughter was born, the baby was a little twisted lump of flesh. There was so much wrong with her that the doctors didn't know where to start. Signora Roversi, realizing that there was only one way of dealing with the situation, took the baby to church with her one day and dumped her in Padre Pio's lap. 'There you are,' she said, '*you* do something. I am not taking her back until you've straightened her out.'

"'What are you doing?' squeaked Padre Pio in great alarm. 'Take this child away at once!'

"'No, I'm leaving her with you until she's cured,' said the mother firmly.

"Well, after that, there was little Padre Pio could do short of a quick miracle," says Father Joseph. "When you see that girl today, she's tall and straight and looks like an Amazon. She leads a perfectly normal life. [The girl, when I see her later at Signora Roversi's, is indeed tall, slim and supple as a reed.]

"I like that story," continues Father Joseph, "because it is so encouraging to parents of children with birth defects. Also, it ties in with what happened to Padre Pio when he was a little boy of five. His father took him one day to the shrine of a saint. As he knelt there, fervently saying his prayers, a woman suddenly flounced in and dumped a child on the altar. The baby, a mongoloid, uttered hideous, blood-curdling croaks. The distracted mother shouted in desperation, 'I can't take care of a child like this. *You* look after it.' As she turned to leave, the baby called out 'mama!' Overjoyed and weeping with happiness, she picked it up. It was perfectly normal. Some say this was Padre Pio's first miracle, but he disclaimed it, attributing it to the saint whose shrine it was."

Father Joseph then tells us the story of Dr. Millilo, the plastic surgeon at the clinic here. Once, when the doctor was in Milan, he had a brain hemorrhage and was rushed to the hospital. The doctors decided he must undergo surgery. But Dr. Millilo insisted on talking to Padre Pio first. He rang up the friary and Padre Pellegrino answered. Just then, Padre Pio walked past. "One moment, padre," said his colleague, "this is Dr. Millilo calling from Milan. He says the doctors want to operate on his brain."

"Tell them to operate on their own brains, and that he is to get out of that hospital at once," snapped Padre Pio, walking on.

Hearing this characteristic reply, passed on by Padre

Pellegrino, Dr. Millilo rang up his wife and asked her to come collect him. When she arrived, the lobby of the hospital was full of his colleagues nervously lurking around the pillars, quite certain he would drop dead before he got to the door. Instead he calmly walked to the car, to be whisked home by his wife. A week later he was back in San Giovanni on duty.

"Then there is the story of the pope's letter. That one has never been published before.

"Pope John Paul II was, at that time, the bishop of Cracow. In 1962, he came to San Giovanni on a visit. After he got home he wrote Padre Pio, in Latin, about a friend of the then pope, a woman doctor and mother of six children, who was dying of cancer. Her condition was terminal, and surgery was considered useless. Padre Pio received hundreds of letters every week, in all languages, but he told his secretary to preserve this one, as well as another, which arrived six weeks later. This second letter, full of fervent thanks, was signed by the father, mother and six children. The doctor was completely healed.

"Another miraculous cure occurred this year when I was in Ireland," continues Father Joseph. "A baby girl was born with a heart murmur and a blockage of the bowel. As she was being rushed to the children's hospital in Dublin, her parents invoked Padre Pio and prayed for the child's recovery. When the X rays and the rest of the tests came up, they were perfectly clear, and there was nothing wrong with the baby."

"So miracles are happening all the time?" I ask.

"They are. What is interesting is what is happening *now*. Padre Pio always insisted his true mission would start after his death."

I ask Father Joseph about Gemma, the blind girl from Sardinia who was said to have been born without pupils in her eyes, and who first saw the light of day when her grandmother brought her to Padre Pio. Once again, the facts are usually reported incorrectly: Gemma began to see on the train *on the way* to San Giovanni. When her grandmother asked Padre Pio to perform a miracle for the little girl, he replied, "But she's had it already."

"She is a freak of nature. Her vision is now excellent. The doctors don't understand the case at all. According to them she should be stone blind. There is more in San Giovanni than meets the eye," concludes Father Joseph, pouring us another cup of tea.

"Will you tell us about bilocation?" asks Christine. "Is it true that Padre Pio was often seen in other places, even though he never left the friary?"

"It certainly is. There is, for instance, the story of the Italian general who had lost an important battle in the First World War. Sitting in his tent, crushed by his defeat and the dishonor involved, he pulled out his revolver and was about to blow his brains out when a friar suddenly appeared before him and asked sternly, 'What on earth do you think you're doing?' After listening to his mysterious visitor's persuasive arguments for half an hour, the general, finally resigned to his humiliation, agreed that he must face the facts and live with them. But when the friar left he went outside and collared the sentry.

"'Why did you let that monk through?' he asked. 'I told you to let no one near my tent.'

"'No one went in, sir,' said the sentry.

"Several years later, the general, having come to San Giovanni on pilgrimage, recognized Padre Pio as the friar who had come to his tent. Walking past the general, the padre glanced at him and remarked, 'That was a rough night we had, wasn't it?'"

"What about the story of the bombers diverted in the air over San Giovanni during the last war?" asks Christine.

"Certainly. There is proof of that."

"Is there anybody living now who might have seen it?"

"Yes, there would be, somewhere in America. The bomber pilot, and maybe some of his crew."

"Do you mean to say Padre Pio actually stood up there in the sky, doing traffic control?" I ask, amazed.

"Exactly. American bombers frequently flew in this direction, as there was an ammunition dump close by. But it happened more than once that pilots disobeyed their orders and returned to base without having got rid of their load. The reason for this is given in the records as: 'The vision of a monk standing in the sky, diverting aircraft.'"

As I goggle at him, speechless, he explains that "Padre Pio had guaranteed that no war damage would occur here. So he made sure it didn't. Foggia, down in the plain, was completely flattened."

It was not till some time later that I came across a mention of this incident in John McCaffery's book. Douglas Woodruff, editor of the *Tablet*, the official British Catholic weekly, had been told the story by his friend Lord Eldon. One day, on the train to Foggia, his lordship had met the American squadron leader concerned. "Bombing mission fatigue was a familiar enough phenomenon— even though it had never before been known to take this peculiar form of spotting monks in the clouds," writes John McCaffery. The squadron leader was worried about the state of his mental faculties, until an Italian orderly told him about Padre Pio and the things he sometimes got up to. So as soon as he was discharged from the U.S. Army Air Corps, the officer, who wanted to get to the bottom of the affair, found his way to San Giovanni and tackled Padre Pio, who confirmed the truth of the story.

Also on the subject of bilocation, the American radio priest, the Reverend Charles Carty, reports a conversation that took place in the padre's cell with Dr. Sanguinetti, director and chief physician in Padre Pio's hospital.

> Dr. Sanguinetti: Padre, when God sends a saint, for instance Saint Anthony, on bilocation, is that person aware of it?
> Padre Pio: Yes. One moment he is here, and the next moment he is where God wants him to be.
> Dr. Sanguinetti: But is he really in two places at once?
> Padre Pio: Yes.
> Dr. Sanguinetti: How is that possible?
> Padre Pio: By a prolongation of the personality.

This argument seems to have satisfied Dr. Sanguinetti, but it leaves me no wiser than before. In San Giovanni nobody would ever dream of questioning it. They talk of Padre Pio going off on bilocation as if he were traveling by bus or train.

In the early days, before pilgrims began to arrive by the thousands, the padre would devote an hour or two every week to his feminine supporters, the Little Flowers, and they would sit around him, discussing spiritual matters. It was a happy time of relaxation for all. But sometimes, without warning, he would suddenly sink into himself and become abstracted. The Little Flowers, who knew what was going on, would wait patiently for his return. "Where have you been this time?" they would ask. Although he didn't usually answer, he did on one occasion sheepishly admit, "Actually, I've just been to see my father and brother in New York, and I called on my sister on the way back" (this sister was a nun in Rome).

Padre Eusebio, who assisted Padre Pio in the last years of his life, said to him one evening as he was helping him get ready for bed, "Bon voyage, padre."

"Thank you," replied Padre Pio calmly.

"Couldn't I hitch a lift with you one night if we tied our cords together?"

"And what if the knot came undone while we were up there?" the padre inquired.

Padre Pio frequently joked about his night visits. When he first arrived in San Giovanni, where there was no plumbing, household slops were frequently flung out of the windows at night. One morning, as the padre and the gardener were chatting in the orchard of the friary, Padre Pio said, "That was a nice perfume you sprinkled over me last night as I passed under your window."

"And now, father, what about your own story?" I ask. "How did you get here, all the way from New York?"

"Rather unusual for a young American to wind up in a Franciscan friary in the wilds of the Apulian mountains, isn't it?" puts in Christine.

"Well, it all began back in 1959, before I had any notion of taking holy orders," he says. "I decided to go on a tour of Europe, and when I was booking for Naples and Rome, the travel agent said, 'Don't you want to go see Padre Pio when you're there?' I had heard friends talk about him, so I said, 'Okay, why not?'"

"So I booked a hotel room in Foggia. While I was having dinner in the hotel, I suddenly felt a tremendous urge to go there right away. I got the driver to take me up the mountain; it was much farther away than I expected, and my itinerary allowed me only one day to see the place.

"That evening I had to push on," continues Father Joseph. "Well, I can tell you it was almost a penance being in Naples and Capri and so forth. I couldn't get Padre Pio out of my head. He was like a magnet, always pulling me back. So I canceled part of my stay in Rome and came here for a couple of weeks. Again I was very happy, although I still hadn't had any direct communication with the padre."

At the end of his tour, Bill, as he was known then, returned to America. Five years later he was in Europe again, and as soon as he could, he rented a car and drove to San Giovanni, where, as before, he regularly attended Padre Pio's 5:00 A.M. masses. A remarkable old woman named Mary Pyle, who was close to the padre, in the course of her confession asked that he accept Bill as his spiritual child. He assented. "And when my time was up I didn't want to go back home," Father Joseph says. "I tell you, I found more peace and contentment in this place than anywhere else in the world.

"I should tell you something about Mary Pyle," the young priest continues. "Padre Pio depended on her a lot. She was born in New Jersey in 1888 into a family of wealthy Presbyterians, but as a young woman she converted to Catholicism and took the name Mary. Then, hearing of Padre Pio, she came here and settled down, as it turned out, for life. She became a tertiary, and the heart and soul of the third order for girls. Having inherited a fortune from her father, she was able to build a church and friary at Pietrelcina, on the spot where the padre had heard church bells as a boy. Mary was his very first helper from abroad, and a wonderfully effective one. She loved music, and she founded a choir here. When she died at the age of eighty, Padre Pio said, 'Now at last she can hear the music of the angels without having to play the organ.'"

Father Joseph pauses to collect his thoughts. "I stayed in San Giovanni the whole of that winter, reading," he says. "Someone suggested that I ask Padre Pio if it was the will of God that I remain in San Giovanni for good. To the interpreter who posed the question, Padre Pio declared very firmly, 'He *shall* stay here. Not he may or he can, but he *shall*.' The friar who was acting as the go-between remarked that it wasn't exactly a place for tourists.

"'It isn't a place for bad people either,' retorted Padre Pio. 'He *shall* stay here.'

"Then he gave me his hand to kiss," says Father Joseph, "and I realized this was the place for me."

By the time spring came around, however, Bill felt restless. So with Padre Pio's permission, he went off to the Holy Land. Bill then visited Istanbul and Greece, but felt so unsettled he cut his stay short and returned to San Giovanni.

He returned during the feast of the Madonna delle Grazie without having planned it so, and the minute he was there, he knew he was home again. "Everywhere else, I was a fish out of water," he says. Having arrived in July, he stayed on until autumn, by which time he felt very sure of his vocation. He decided he must go back to America to pursue his goal. Having packed his bags, he asked Padre Eusebio to act as his interpreter in requesting Padre Pio's blessing.

"The next day was the feast of Saint Francis, and Padre Eusebio came to me and said, 'Padre Pio says you are to stay here.'" Although he didn't know what to make of this, Bill felt a surge of relief. "It was all right by me," he says. "I thought, fine, as long as he accepts the responsibility before God for me to stay here and not follow my vocation as I feel I should, then I'm only too happy to stay."

A few months later he found himself installed in the friary without really quite knowing how it had happened. And he remained there as a third-order Franciscan until the death of Padre Pio. Once, when he had just been clothed in the third-order habit, he was sitting on the verandah with Padre Pio. Feeling infinitely happy and full of the peace of God, he was wondering whom he should thank for this grace, the Blessed Virgin or the padre. And without a word being uttered on the subject, the padre looked at him and said, *"La Madonna."* Another time, when Bill was making an offering of money, the padre asked sharply, "Where did you get that from?"

"From my parents," he answered.

"I know," says Father Joseph, "that Padre Pio wanted me to realize that this money that I had inherited was due to my father's hard work."

The day after Padre Pio asked about Bill's money, the two were again sitting on the verandah together when the padre suddenly told him, out of the blue, "The souls of your parents are blessed in heaven."

"My desire to become a priest was really his last gift to me," says Father Joseph. In order to follow his mentor as closely as possible, Bill went to the novitiate on the same day Padre Pio had entered—January 3.

After tea, Christine and I stroll along the corridors in the wake of Father Joseph, who shows us into another small parlor. Furnished with an oilcloth-covered table and a few chairs, it is as austere as all the others.

"This is the guest dining room of the friary," says our host as we settle down around the table. Then he resumes his stories. "One evening when Padre Raffaele was entertaining his sister at dinner," he tells us, "Padre Pio dropped by here to say hello to her. Before leaving, she decided to pay a visit to the Blessed Sacrament, and her brother went with her. Padre Pio was left alone in the parlor. All at once, he looked up and saw a stranger standing in front of him, surprising since all the doors were locked for the night.

"'Who are you?' asked Padre Pio.

"'I am so-and-so,' said the man. 'I was born in such-and-such a place.' And he gave his parents' names as well, by way of introduction. 'I lived here during the suppression,' he added, 'and I am doing my purgatory.'

"I believe he had killed a man," says Father Joseph.

"'What?' said Padre Pio. 'Doing your purgatory!' He hadn't realized he was talking to an apparition. At this point the man vanished.

"When Padre Pio told him the story, Padre Raffaele went to the town hall to consult the archives. Everything the man had divulged checked out—his name and those of his parents were in the records. Padre Pio said a mass for his visitor, who was never seen again."

We are now on our way out, back in all those interminable corridors.

"I'll tell you another story of something that happened during the First World War," continues our guide. "The main door of the friary was always closed for the night when the Angelus bell rang, and the iron bars were placed in such a way that the doors couldn't be forced open. One evening, Padre Raffaele, who was superior at the time, heard voices in the corridor, shouting, 'Viva Padre Pio! Viva Padre Pio!' He called the porter, Padre Gerardo, and said, 'Someone's got in, and there are people yelling in the hallway. Get them out and close those doors.'

"'The doors were locked,' Padre Gerardo reported when he came back. 'The metal arms are in place, and there is no one in the hall.'

"Padre Raffaele was puzzled, but knowing as he did that around Padre Pio you could expect all sorts of extraordinary happenings, he had his suspicions. The next morning he asked the padre, 'Do you know anything about the yelling in the corridor last night, after everything was locked up?'

"'Oh, yes,' the young friar replied, 'they were the souls of the dead soldiers who were here to thank me for my prayers.' And he added, 'There are more souls of the dead coming up that road to ask for my prayers than souls of the living.'"

We chew this over for a while, visualizing the endless procession of suffering souls surging up the ancient mule track and floating onto the piazza.

"He was living in another dimension," continues Father Joseph, "with one foot here and the other in the supernatural world. He maintained a perfect balance, and never let you know what was going on.

"One day, in this very hall, a woman whose son had recently died came up to him. She said, 'Padre, please tell me if my son is in heaven.' And he flashed back, as sharp as ever, 'Why, yes, I've just come from there myself, this very moment.'"

There was a story which, according to Father Joseph, Padre Pio loved to tell. It was about an old peasant who decided one day to take a trip on a train. This was at the beginning of the century, when the railway was still an exciting novelty. The old boy went to the station and asked the clerk for a round-trip ticket.

"Where do you want to go?" the clerk asked.

"Well, really, I don't see that this has anything to do with you," answered the old man indignantly.

"When do you want to leave?"

"I would have thought that was *my* business, not yours," said the would-be traveler, quite huffily by now.

With much tact and patience, the clerk managed to explain the mysteries of this novel form of travel to the old peasant, and a trip was worked out for him.

Came the day, and he boarded his train with some trepidation.

As it started to pick up speed, the noise struck terror into his heart. He clung to his seat for safety. Opposite him sat a man observing these symptoms with some amusement.

Suddenly the speeding train plunged into a tunnel. Huge clouds of sulphurous smoke invaded the compartment and sparks flew past the windows. The racket was deafening.

"Where are we? What's happening now?" yelled the terrified old peasant.

"Just entering hell," answered his companion.

"Oh, that's all right, then," said the old boy, with relief. "I've got a return ticket."

A POWERHOUSE
OF PRAYER

LIDÉ WAS ONE OF PADRE PIO'S EARLIEST SPIRITUAL
daughters and one of his staunchest Little Flowers.
As we sip coffee with her one afternoon, our hostess mentions a respectable elder of the town known simply as Pietruccio, and my sister's eyes light up.

"Since you know Pietruccio so well, why don't you
ask *him* to tell us his story?" Christine asks.

"Certainly," Elidé agrees. "I will ring him up at
once."

A long telephone conversation follows, but from
what I can make out, it doesn't seem to be going too
well. "I tell you she is not a journalist," Elidé is saying
very firmly. "She is writing a book, not a feature for a
newspaper." In the end she slams the receiver down in
exasperation. "It's no good," she says. "I've done my
best, but he absolutely refuses to see you."

"What was all that about a journalist?" I ask.

"It seems that one of those gentlemen once twisted
or misunderstood something Pietruccio told him, and he
won't have anything to do with scribblers anymore."

I groan, and heave a heavy sigh.

"But he says you are welcome to use the little book
he wrote himself."

Feeling thankful for small mercies, I trot along to the bookshop, where the only available copy of Pietruccio's opus turns out to be in German. I buy it and eventually manage to persuade my husband to translate it for me, and when we get back to the south of France, the two of us spend many a painstaking afternoon by the fire, struggling with the Teutonic text.

For better or for worse, this is what we make of Pietruccio's story.

Pietruccio, who has been blind since he was a child, remembers San Giovanni as a village entirely cut off from the rest of the world. Two miles from his home was the friary, which was to become the center of his world, and the little church of Santa Maria delle Grazie.

The country churches of southern Italy have a flat, undecorated face, with a plain wooden door and a single bell hanging in the belfry. You never see a spire in this part of the world. The dour and rugged character of the inhabitants is reflected in the severe appearance and total lack of ornament of their churches. Mountain people are notoriously withdrawn, secretive, suspicious of foreigners and harsh with one another. Their whole lives are dedicated to God, and to Him they give everything in full measure. The natives of San Giovanni are typical of this "otherworld outlook." When you know that the Madonna is walking the streets of your village, that the souls of the dead are trooping up the mule track day in and day out to beg Padre Pio for his prayers and that the altar steps are crowded with shining angels at mass every morning, this knowledge is bound to color your approach and direct your thoughts toward the supernatural all through the day.

So San Giovanni Rotondo is, in effect, a powerhouse of prayer. It is like a very strong cell in an enormous organism that is slowly dying of a pernicious disease. From this mighty spiritual center, Padre Pio sent out a network

SANTA MARIA DELLE GRAZIE TODAY. THE ORIGINAL FRI-
ARY CHURCH IS LEFT OF THE TREE.

of other healing cells all through the afflicted body of the world in the form of his prayer groups.

Padre Pio established the first of these prayer groups in 1947. By the time he died in 1968 there were more than seven hundred in existence. Now there are over a thousand throughout the planet, with new ones forming all the time. Over and over again Padre Pio said it was by prayer alone that the world could be saved. He himself, who never stopped praying, gave constant warnings of what would happen if people persistently ignored his appeal. He came as a kind of last chance, holding back the threatening arm of God with one hand, while frantically beckoning humanity with the other, to "Come in, hurry, get back into the fold before it is too late," as he put it.

In 1920, when Pietruccio was six years old, he rode on his father's shoulders to his first visit to Padre Pio. Appearing at the little choir window of the church, the padre blessed the assembled faithful, who asked for help and graces of every kind. He always said, "Pray, and I will also pray."

From the time news of the stigmata got around, Padre Pio was clamored for every hour of the day. Everybody wanted to see him, have a word with him, kiss his hand. People came from miles around on foot, by mule, in horse carts and broken-down old trucks.

In the morning the padre would enter the sacristy with two friars and two carabinieri following behind. He stood on a low wooden platform to avoid being crushed by the crowds. Although the people had to keep moving, they all insisted on kissing his poor, bleeding hands and telling him of their needs.

Sometimes, in the summer, the heat became so oppressive that his asthma nearly choked him. At such moments, resorting to levitation, he would calmly step over the heads of the faithful and slip outside for a reviving breath of air. "Where is the padre?" the people would ask. The next instant, to their uncomprehending astonishment, he was back on his platform.

Shepherds brought their flocks, and farmers their horses and donkeys, to be blessed. Pietruccio was often dispatched to help herd the animals onto the piazza. After lunch, the padre came out on the square and sat on the little wall opposite the church, to chat with the people who came there to chew their tough country bread and onions.

At 1:30, when the bell rang for silence, the padre returned to his cell to pray and work, after which he went to the choir. In winter, when the cold was piercing, he would pull his hood over his head. People often said that when he was immersed in prayer he glowed with a strange fluorescent light, and that heat radiated out of his habit. After this, he would go down into the church to hear confessions. Everybody wanted to confess to him, and until the booking system was instituted, there was always a frenzied scramble. During recreation he often sat in the almond orchard, spinning endless yarns to the delight of the other friars and his spiritual sons.

Pietruccio began to lose his sight when he was twelve. First a red band appeared before his eyes; then came a bright light followed by a fiery red color. He could still just make out the shapes of people around him.

One day, his father took him to Padre Pio. Concerned, the padre had one of his spiritual daughters, a woman named Angela, take the boy to a doctor. "We need an oculist," this man told her. So Pietruccio and his father went to Bari for three weeks to consult with Professor Durante.

Pietruccio does not tell us what treatment he received. All we know is that he returned to San Giovanni with his sight restored. On a very cold evening in March, a bonfire was burning in honor of the Feast of the Annunciation. A circus had arrived in town, and Pietruccio and his friends were larking around, peeking through a hole in a circus tent, then jumping forward and backward across the fire. As he jumped, the red veil suddenly swept across his vision again, and he had to be led home. His father took him once more to Padre Pio.

The padre asked the boy, "But, Pietro, do you want to see again, or don't you?"

"If sight is the best thing for my soul," the boy replied, "then may the Lord give it back to me, together with the grace to achieve eternal salvation and to live as a good Christian. However, if it is going to be bad for my soul, I would rather stay blind."

"But you yourself, don't you want to see again?"

"No."

Padre Pio could not understand this at all. "But do you want to see or don't you want to see?" he persisted.

"No, padre. I am happy as I am, and even if it gets

worse, the most important thing for me is to save my soul."

"Hmm, do you hear that? He doesn't want his sight back!"

"Padre, it isn't so. I don't want it if it is going to endanger my salvation."

The padre brought the subject up again and again. He couldn't get over it.

"Just look how happy he is. And he doesn't want his sight back. . . ."

"But, padre, if the Lord takes it in atonement for my sins, then I am content, and I shall go on feeling like this as long as I can be near you. For me you are life. It is essential that I should always be allowed to be near you."

"Ah, Pietro, you've got it good."

"How so, padre?"

"Because you can't see the wickedness of this world."

"Padre, I am happy to be with you, and my cross, compared with yours, is nothing."

"So you are really happy?"

"Yes, I am happy."

The padre was always coming back to this subject. Was he, perhaps, giving Pietruccio a chance to ask for a miracle? But the boy never did. Instead, he said, "Padre, ask Jesus to let me die before you."

"Hmm. Why? You're just a young chap."

"How could I manage without you? Coming to the friary would be a terrible pain. You are the whole of my life."

In the early 1930s, when Padre Pio was a virtual prisoner in the friary, the teenaged Pietruccio was not entirely cut off from him. During those two years, the padre spent long hours reading and studying in the library, and there the blind boy, slipping in unobtrusively, would find him, and bring him news of the village and of his spiritual children. Pietruccio, whose whole heart was in

PADRE PIO AND ITALIAN OPERA SINGER BENIAMINO GIGLI
IN THE FRIARY GARDEN.

the friary, made himself useful to its occupants. Twice a
day he took their mail up to them and he did their shop-
ping. In one way or another, Pietruccio was constantly
and happily occupied doing little jobs for the friars.

Then came a day of great rejoicing. It was announced that on Sunday, July 16, 1933, Padre Pio would
be allowed to celebrate mass in public again. Pietruccio
was the first to receive Communion from him.

The padre's death, Pietruccio relates in his little book, shattered him completely. He then felt the full weight of his blindness. "I didn't notice it before, because it was he who was bearing my cross. I even used to thank God for being blind. He gave me so many graces that others didn't have. I could go to the padre's cell whenever I wanted. Nobody ever tried to stop me or keep me away from him. Sometimes Padre Pio said, 'You lend me your arm, and I will lend you my eyes,' and I would help him to Padre Agostino's cell, or wherever he wanted to go. And he told the doctors who were visiting him one night, 'This is the hour when I can't stand on my own feet, and I get fainting fits. So Pietruccio helps me.'"

Pietruccio would stay until Padre Pio got into bed, then kneel beside him for his blessing and kiss his hand. "I was brimming with joy when I left him. For it was enough to be near him, and a single word or gesture would make me ecstatic with joy," he writes, and goes on, "I would leap with joy in the morning, just at the thought of embracing him. I rushed from the house without difficulty and ran faster than a man with two good eyes, rain or shine. As soon as I was in his presence, joy filled my soul. To be at the altar, hearing his mass, was as though a miracle had happened to me. And now what is left?"

A few days before his death, Padre Pio came out to the verandah with Father Joseph. As he walked past Pietruccio, he said, "Good night, Pietro. I am sorry, but I have to leave you." Pietruccio then understood how very ill he was.

"But, padre," he said helplessly, "let us pray that the Lord . . ."

"Eh, I must leave you," was all he said.

These were his last words to Pietruccio.

· 10 ·

THE RELUCTANT
DISCIPLE

C LOSE TO THE FRIARY CHURCH IN SAN GIOVANNI IS
    a spacious, comfortable guest house. Always
    packed, in or out of season, it seems to shelter
even more animals than human beings. On the doorstep
as we arrive sits a beautiful Alsatian puppy, fit and
healthy-looking as an advertisement for dog food.

"They are potty about dogs and cats here," says
Christine. "They have so many animals already that they
want me to take this one," she says, pointing at the
frisky-looking pup who thumps his tail and flicks his
tongue mischievously. "But I'm afraid poor Mini would
go mad if I did," she adds. Yes, it would mean another
nervous breakdown, I shouldn't wonder.

Surrounded by yelping dogs, Peppina, the maid,
opens the door and lets us in. I gather from Christine
that the girl roams the countryside in her free time looking for abandoned animals and spends most of her wages
feeding her menagerie and having hopeless cases hu-
manely put down by the vet in Foggia.

The horde of boisterous hounds bounces and leaps
around us, as rowdy as any medieval hunting pack.
Swarming all over the dining room, they finally come to
roost in their own self-appointed places as we wait for
our hostess to arrive.

Still in her working clothes, Signora Gianina comes in wearing an apron and a scarf over her short, gray hair. An enormous kind of poodle creature follows her in, leaps at each one of us in turn, then buries his head in her lap. They have a prolonged cuddle. "We love each other very much," she says. I rejoice at the sight, a most unusual one in this country. But she is not, at first, so friendly to me.

"Why do you want to know about Padre Pio?" she asks suspiciously. Finally she seems to accept my accustomed spiel and embarks on her story, gradually warming to it as her memories come flooding back.

To begin with, it was thanks to her aunt Melita that Gianina was in San Giovanni.

Back in the year 1920, Zia Melita, who was eighteen and living in Turin, heard about the young friar who had received the stigmata in the wilds of the Gargano mountains, in the south of Italy. She decided to check out the truth of the story herself. So she packed a bag and set off across the land, changing trains here and there on the way, until she got to Foggia. In those days it was pretty unusual for girls of her age to travel about the countryside on their own. But she was a determined and independent young person, and nobody could stand in her way.

At Foggia, Melita climbed aboard a decrepit old stage coach, as there was no other way of getting up the mountain. Bumping along the tortuous mule track through the barren countryside, it took twelve hours to reach San Giovanni. Along the route, bandits would lie in wait for the Foggia coach. They regarded the passengers' money and valuables as lawful pickings, and stealing them a perfectly respectable way of earning a living. Any girl in the coach they fancied they kidnapped as well, this being their only means of "persuading" women to share their savage existence in the mountains.

These brigands lived in the caves that honeycombed the mountains, and they alone knew where the underground passages started, joined up with one another and resurfaced. Anybody else venturing into them would get lost and never be seen again. Once back in their lairs, the bandits were perfectly safe. No carabinieri, they knew, would ever be bold enough to follow them.

Melita's angel was watching over her on that coach trip up the mountain. She arrived in San Giovanni safely. She soon realized, however, that there was no place for her to stay. A few stone hovels stood about, crumbling and forlorn. There were no streets, no lights, no plumbing of any kind. In the end, she prevailed upon one of the local families to take her in. In the middle of the only ground-floor room, she found members of the family sitting around the usual charcoal brazier, chatting, knitting, snoozing or telling their beads. Over the brazier stood a hob on which dinner was cooked. In those days it would consist of lentils, beans, chickpeas or green vegetables— one at a time, of course, not all together. (Pasta was only for the rich, and a Sunday treat at that, while meat was unheard of.) When Melita was asked what she would like for supper, she tentatively suggested soup, if that wasn't asking too much. So soup it was. As the pot was duly placed over the embers, the mother sat going through her young daughter's hair, picking out the nits and dropping them into the fire. Fearing that some might land in the soup, Melita kept a close and apprehensive watch over the proceedings.

After dinner, everybody trooped off to the one upstairs room. It contained two beds, and with touching hospitality Melita's hosts offered her the larger one to herself. "Let me have the girls, at least," Melita protested. When she drew back the bedclothes, however, she couldn't help noticing that the sheets were dirty. "Those are only the marks left by bedbugs," answered the mistress of the house. "What do you expect?"

In the middle of the floor stood a bucket, which everybody used in turn. Some time during the night, a cart trundled past, ringing a bell to wake the good people of San Giovanni from their bug-ridden slumbers. The mother seized the pail and hurried downstairs to empty its contents into the waiting cart. Such was San Giovanni in 1920.

By 1922, Padre Pio's fame was spreading apace. People came on foot, on mule-back and in carts, from all over Italy. At the padre's suggestion, Melita bought a plot of land near the friary, and built a guest house upon it to accommodate the ever-increasing flood of pilgrims. When this was full up they camped in the field, and the biblical landscape around the friary was soon peppered with tents. It was then that the Vatican authorities began to take notice. The stigmata, and the increasing numbers of pilgrims, roused their suspicions about a cause that hadn't received the stamp of their approval. An emissary was despatched to bring the young friar back to Rome, where they could keep an eye on him and make up their own minds about the quality of his sanctity.

The unhappy bishop to whom this task fell set off on the long journey. As he was bouncing along in the creaking old *carozza* on his way up the mountain, the horses suddenly reared and the coach nearly overturned. Seconds later, the curtains were wrenched apart and a scowling, bearded face peered inside.

The bandits were at it again. But this time they were not after loot or women. Having heard of the bishop's coming, they wanted to give him due warning. "If you try to take Padre Pio away," the man growled, "we will shoot him out of hand, and you can take a corpse away with you. He will never leave this place alive. So be warned." And whipping their mounts, they galloped off.

But this did not end the affair. The provincial of the Franciscan order arrived from Foggia with Padre Benedetto, Padre Pio's spiritual director. This time the bandits had recruited reinforcements from the village, and the friary was surrounded by the threatening multitude.

Shaken by these demonstrations, the heads of the church decided not to endanger the young Capuchin's life. The father guardian produced and read aloud a signed declaration promising that Padre Pio would not be moved. On hearing this, the mob calmed down and dispersed; but for the next few days, just to be sure, patrols kept watch at key positions, communicating with one another by means of smoke signals.

Instead of taking the young friar away, the Holy See decided to lock him up in his monastery, where he could no longer see or speak to anyone, or even hear confessions.

He was forbidden to show his stigmata to anyone— let alone have them kissed—or even to talk about them. He was no longer allowed to say mass in public or give anyone his blessing. Moreover, he was asked to make a formal statement that all he wanted was to be left in peace to attend to his own salvation. Padre Pio was, in fact, a prisoner, and this in spite of the fact that Pope Benedict XV declared him in the same year to be one of those rare men God sends down once in a while to save souls.

Little by little, the disappointed pilgrims dropped away and the excitement died down. But two years later the local people began to agitate for their padre to say mass for them again. This time, three thousand people, headed by the mayor and backed by the military, surrounded the friary. So the provincial, who didn't want a revolution on his hands, agreed to allow public mass again. From the moment this was announced, Padre Pio was allowed to resume a normal Franciscan life and could even hear confessions.

From then on, until 1933, restrictions were brought to bear over and over again, from both inside and outside the church. Difficulties of every kind, calumnies, prohibitions, and endless torments, were inflicted on the poor priest, whose one aim was to offer himself as a victim for the souls of the ungrateful human race, including those of his tormentors. Even now, people who witnessed these events find tears welling to their eyes as they talk about them.

From the very outset, Padre Pio gradually gathered a band of loyal followers. Inevitably, there were bruised feelings and even jealousy among them. In those early days Padre Pio still had time to give them each an hour a week. If he gave a minute longer to one, the others were disturbed and upset. During these sessions they discussed their spiritual life with him and received his advice. Later, he could only do this in the confessional.

On one occasion, the young padre said to Zia Melita, one of the first of his spiritual children, "Come into the sacristy, Melita, and sit there quietly. Just watch and listen." And in a few more minutes, in minced one of the spiritual daughters, the one who habitually took up so much of the young Capuchin's time. After kneeling for his blessing and kissing his hand, she began to chatter. For over an hour she shamelessly wasted the padre's time with her senseless inanities. In her corner, Zia Melita understood the lesson. "Poor padre, poor padre," she kept saying to herself. And when the featherbrain finally left, they looked at each other.

"I just have to put up with it. She is one of my flock, part of my cross," his eyes were saying.

Zia Melita was supposed to go to a job in a girls' home in Jerusalem, but Padre Pio required her services in San Giovanni. When the Patriarch of Jerusalem heard of this, he wrote, "Obey the dictates of a saint." And from that moment on she never again left the village on the mountain.

Melita's niece, Gianina, had been hearing about the padre since earliest childhood. She had always received a great deal of devoted attention from her various aunts, and she admits herself that she grew up a spoiled and willful child. But Melita always spoke of her to Padre Pio with the greatest pride. Every two years her photograph was taken and duly mailed to him. "As I grew up," says Gianina, "I got the feeling that my life was entirely controlled by this monk. He even announced that he approved of my pigtails." When she was fifteen, it was decided to send her off to San Giovanni so that Melita could present her to the padre. She said she didn't want to go, but no notice was taken. Her mother took her to the station, bought a ticket and put her on the train to Foggia.

"I was crying so much that she eventually took pity on me and let me off before the train left," says Gianina. "But five years later the subject came up again and there was no way of putting it off."

But she took care to go to confession before leaving, as she had heard that the padre didn't take penitents less than ten days after their last absolution. She assumed she would therefore be sent packing and be safely home again before the regulation ten days were up. On the morning after her arrival, Zia Melita took her to church, explaining the seating. To keep bickering to a minimum, the faithful had been split into two groups: the locals on one side of the church and the "foreigners" (from surrounding villages and outlying towns) on the other. Though told to join the local group, out of pigheadedness, Gianina sat with the foreign detachment.

When her turn for confession came, she informed Padre Pio that she had been to her own priest at home the previous day, expecting him to tell her to come back in ten days' time. Instead, he murmured in the gentlest possible way, "At last you have come!"

"But you don't know me!" said Gianina in surprise.

"Don't I just! 'I don't want to go! I don't want to go!'" he mimicked. "Even when your mother had put you on the train, you still managed to get home again! You didn't want to come to me, so I had to go to you. You see, I do know you."

Even though Gianina was shaken by these revelations, she refused to thaw. There was no shame or repentance in her heart. With infinite gentleness, Padre Pio said, finally, "Will you at least allow me to give you absolution?"

This took her so much by surprise that she couldn't think of a reason to refuse.

"Will you wait for me under the arch?" he asked.

"No," said Gianina, but he insisted so much that at last she agreed. Arriving at their rendezvous, he invited her to sit down. "I felt all the fascination of his saintly presence," she says now, "but at that moment I knew quite well that the slightest show of obedience on my part would have meant unconditional surrender. And I wanted my freedom, not renunciation, sacrifice and everything that goes with a Christian way of life."

"Sit down," he told her again.

But Gianina knew that in the presence of a saint you either stand or kneel, but never sit.

"No, I don't want to," she snapped.

Quietly the padre took a chair and sat down.

"You can ask me whatever you want, anything you like," he said slowly.

This was a terrible moment for Gianina. After a silence which seemed to her an eternity, and to her amazement and horror, she heard herself say, "To stay with you always, padre." Slowly he stood up and said, placing his hand on her head, "This is what I wanted from you." Then, walking slowly toward the friary door, he disappeared.

This made her so angry that she went off in a rage. The next day she left for Turin, furious with herself. It was ten years before she returned to San Giovanni. During all that time she carefully stayed away from church, fearing that the mere sight of a priest would remind her of Padre Pio. She knew he would then start controlling her life again.

Finally, while the war was raging, Gianina, in Rome with her sister-in-law, suddenly found herself on her knees, overwhelmed by an irresistible longing for San Giovanni. The next day her mind was full of the place, and she felt herself compulsively drawn there.

The following day, Gianina got on the train to Foggia. Having bumped her way up the mountain track in the ancient *carozza*, she was greeted by her aunt, who was overjoyed to see her.

At five the next morning Gianina went to mass, throughout which she sat in a trance. "I caught the padre's eye and he held my gaze for I don't know how long," she says. "In those days, mass went on for three or four hours." (This eventually had to be reduced to one and a half hours, as people were constantly in trouble with their employers for arriving late at work.) Padre Pio's mass was a transcendental affair that often reduced people to tears. "We really felt we were taking part in the sacrifice he offered on the altar," says Gianina. "He used to glance at one of us, and then another, until everybody was included and had added his or her part to his own sublime performance." People sometimes saw the blood of the passion trickling down his forehead.

One girl, engaged to a young man whose faith had lapsed, threatened that she wouldn't marry him unless he returned to the Church. She lured him to Padre Pio's mass. Standing there, watching the altar, the young man became more and more absorbed, concerned and stricken.

"It is always like that?" he asked.

"Yes," said his fiancée, unaware that he was looking at the crown of thorns squashed down over Padre Pio's head—actually a great mass of brambles in no way resembling the delicately plaited strands of spikes and thorns traditionally painted by artists.

After mass, on that first day of her return, Gianina joined the crowds in the corridor through which the padre walked on the way back to his cell. There she knelt with the others to receive his blessing. When he reached her, he put his hand on her head.

"'So this little head is back again,' he said as he blessed me."

Staring at Gianina as she pronounces these words, my eyes almost pop out of their sockets. The scarf is no longer on her head, and her face is framed instead in the soft, fringed style Ingrid Bergman wore as Joan of Arc. And the lined skin is now smooth as a girl's. I glance at her shoulders to see if the scarf has slipped down, but there is no sign of it. When I look up again, it is back in place, and the short gray hair once more bristles on the lined forehead. Hallucinations, I say to myself. Watch out!

Soon after his blessing, Gianina's mother wrote asking her daughter to come home. But instead the girl, who no longer wanted to leave, asked her mother to send her clothes to her. When the mother refused and became ill, Gianina went to Padre Pio to ask for his blessing.

"Don't go," he said. "You're to stay here."

"But, padre, my mother is ill. I must go and look after her."

"Your mother's fever has left her. She even went out for a walk this afternoon and sat on a bench in the sun for fifteen minutes."

When her mother heard that, she remarked, "This man is a saint." Soon afterward she had a dream, from which she gathered that her death was approaching. She traveled to San Giovanni, to tell Padre Pio that she still had some business on earth to straighten out.

"Well," he told her, "I will ask the Lord to prolong your life just a *little*."

The Lord claimed her soon after that, but not before she had been granted extra time.

· 11 ·

ELIDE

W HEN ELIDÉ AS A VERY YOUNG WOMAN FIRST
came to San Giovanni in 1946, there were
only four friars in the convent besides Padre
Pio, the five of them rattling around in that huge building, with all those endless icy corridors.

Elidé had come from Sestri Levante, on the west
coast of Italy, where she lived with her widowed mother
and her aunt who was incurably ill. Lying on her sick-
bed, the aunt was always in tears. She talked continually
about somebody called Padre Pio.

"If only I could let him know how frightened I am of
dying," she sobbed. "I pray God lets me die without my
knowing it."

One day, Elidé, who couldn't bear her aunt's misery
any longer, said to her mother, "I am going to see this
Padre Pio she is always talking about."

"You can't possibly go so far by yourself."

But Elidé stuck to her guns. Her father had worked
for the railways, leaving her a lifelong free pass, so off
she went, bound for the south. By the time she finally
reached Foggia it was dark and very late. She set off on
foot through the bomb-ravaged city in search of a convent or a hotel, but found neither. So back to the station
she went. There she sat on her suitcase and burst into

tears. The stationmaster was kind, and he showed her to a little room with a stove in it. "Sit here by the fire and rest," he said. "The bus leaves at 4:00 A.M. I will get somebody to take you to it tomorrow morning."

Next morning, as she climbed aboard the bus, she was almost knocked over by a very strong scent.

"What is this smell?" she asked.

"Ah," the passengers said, "that's the perfume of the padre."

The perfume of the padre? What were they talking about? She took a seat and said no more. In San Giovanni she got out at the last stop, nearest the friary at the top of the hill. The ground was covered with snow. It was late March, and in Sestri Levante, south of Genoa on the Ligurian coast, spring was well on its way. Knowing nothing of the savage climate of the east coast, Elidé had arrived in a silk coat and skirt. Her bare feet were in sandals. But she started up the snow-covered mule tracks, twisting her ankles in the ruts.

Near the friary was a house with rooms to let. The landlady sat Elidé down by the great charcoal brazier in the middle of the kitchen and listened to her story. "Tomorrow you will go to confession to Padre Pio," she said, "and you can tell him about your aunt. Sit by the wall in church, and you will be one of the first to go in."

Next morning in church, the woman ahead of Elidé was being given a rough time.

"Go away," Padre Pio was telling her. "Don't waste my time."

"But, padre, I've come all the way from Switzerland to confess my sins to you."

"And who asked you to come?" he snapped. "Go and put yourself in a state of grace; then we will see." Elidé was quite unnerved. "Goodness," she said to herself, "what kind of confessor is this priest?"

The women behind were pushing her forward. "Go

on," one said, "it's your turn; get on with it." Trembling, she went in. The padre turned to her.

"How long is it since you went to confession?" he asked.

"Just a week, padre. But I am so frightened I can hardly speak."

And so he talked to her as if she were a child. At the end of her confession, Elidé brought up the subject of her aunt.

"Wait," he said. "Say your penance and then we will talk later."

When he had finished with all the confessions, he went to her. "Right. Now you tell me what you have to say." She gave him her aunt's message. "I will bear her in mind," he assured her. "I will pray for you and your aunt."

Suddenly, without knowing why, Elidé asked, "Padre, will you take me on as your spiritual daughter?"

"Most willingly," he answered. "Right away."

"No," she said, "not yet, padre. I have to go home."

"You will live here and work here," he told her bluntly.

"No, no," she cried, horrified. "You will never see me living *here!* I'll ask Jesus to let me die rather than live here."

"Oh, so that's what you think. Don't you know it's the will of God that you should come and live here?"

The will of God! When she heard that she began to cry.

"But I can't come and live here. I want to go back to my mother."

"As for your mother, I will take care of her myself. You will live here and work here," he said firmly. "Don't you know that they have already started the work?" And he pointed at the hospital site. She didn't know they were building a hospital, and she didn't care. She just wanted to get home as quickly as possible. Once more she burst into tears.

"Come here," Padre Pio said kindly, "and I will bless you." He put his hand on her head. "You will live here and work here, and I will take care of your mother myself," he said again.

When she arrived home and blurted out the news, her mother said, "I am sure you misunderstood him. He didn't mean that."

"I think he really did mean it," said Elidé miserably.

A month went by; her aunt was getting worse every day.

"It's obvious that Padre Pio of yours can do nothing for me," she wailed.

One day Elidé announced that she was going back to San Giovanni. There she went to see Padre Pio and repeated what her mother had said.

"Listen to me," he told her firmly. "I will look after your mother myself, and you will stay here and work here."

"But when my mother dies I want to be with her and help her."

"I will take care of that as well," he said.

So she returned home once more, this time feeling a little more resigned to the idea of living in San Giovanni. During her absence, her aunt had died, on the first Friday of the month, which is dedicated to the Sacred Heart of Jesus. On Thursday evening she had asked for her confessor and put her affairs in order. The next morning a priest brought her Communion, and she told her sister to leave her while she did her thanksgiving. "I will call you when I am ready," she added, so she left her alone. But she didn't call, and as time went by, her sister began to worry. "She is taking a deuce of a time over her thanksgiving," she thought. "I'd better go and see what she's up to." She found her dead, smiling as if she had seen the Sacred Heart of Jesus Himself.

Elidé went back to San Giovanni and told Padre Pio her aunt had died. "The Lord in his inscrutable wisdom decided to shorten her sufferings and call her to Himself," he said. "Who knows how much more she would have had to suffer from the tumor? Now she's happy in heaven."

Though Elidé was the right hand of her parish priest, or *parroco*, who depended heavily on her competence and energy, she began to organize pilgrimages to San Giovanni. Her first group consisted of five young men and two young women. One of the boys was a deaf-mute who hoped Padre Pio would cure him. Elidé took him to confession, but the padre made the boy understand by unmistakable signs that he was not in the right frame of mind and would have to prepare himself better. The youth came away shattered. Elidé pushed him in again and tackled the sacristan. "Do try and get it fixed for him," she pleaded. Padre Pio agreed to see him once more on condition that the boy lead a better life. But Elidé wasn't satisfied. She went to see the padre.

"Listen," she said, "don't let me take that boy home like this. Do a miracle and get him cured."

"The Almighty is not going to cure him because he wants to use his faculties for sinful purposes," replied the padre.

And with that Elidé had to be content. However, the young man went home in a new frame of mind. From then on he went to church every Sunday and was seen praying so often that his parents began to fear he was going out of his mind. Far from it. Soon after, he became a tailor and married a very devout girl who was a dressmaker. By the time they had a family of four handsome children, Elidé felt her job was done as far as this particular protégé of hers was concerned.

Elidé was now running pilgrimages to San Giovanni on a regular basis, attracting more and more people. Incensed by her activities on behalf of Padre Pio, some of the local Communists went to see her mother. If she didn't stop Elidé from organizing "those affairs," they threatened to place concealed bombs on the pilgrims' train.

"Do stop this business," she begged her daughter, "or they will kill you."

"In that case," answered Elidé, "I am going to fix up another pilgrimage immediately. The padre will look after us."

Telling this story, Elidé glows with pride. "Just think," she said, "I laid on a pilgrimage for seventy-two people. And we had a Communist with us—he was their standard-bearer." The day before they were due to leave, he went to see Elidé and said, "Signorina, it is twenty-three years since I last went to church and confession."

"I am not interested," she answered. "You go to church tomorrow morning. Leave your party card with the parroco and he will burn it for you. If you don't want to do as I say, go with another pilgrimage. The same goes for everybody else," she added firmly.

Then, striding off to see the parroco herself, she addressed him thus: "Listen to me, monsignore; I am organizing a pilgrimage to San Giovanni Rotondo, and you should come with us, too. You are the pastor of your parishioners."

"You forget that you are the president of the Catholic Action Group, and your place is here in this town. You have no business gallivanting about the country," answered the parroco.

Often before, the parroco had complained to her

mother, "How can you let her go like that? She thinks she is in charge of the whole world. She is a fanatic. Can't you manage to keep her at home?"

Elidé's mother, nagged by the Communists on one hand and the parroco on the other, scolded her daughter nonstop. But Elidé was firm. "Listen to me, mama. It is the will of God. I have to listen to Padre Pio and Our Lord and no one else. Let the parroco come and see for himself."

And so she tackled the parroco. "A Communist is coming with us tomorrow. I told him to bring his party card for you to burn," she told him.

"He has been already," said the priest, defeated. "And we have burnt the card. If you can talk one of those people into it, who am I to say no to you?"

When the group swarmed into San Giovanni, Elidé went to see the sacristan. "Listen," she said to him, "the parroco from my hometown is with us. Have him serve mass for Padre Pio. Then get the padre to give him a really big blessing, for this priest is always telling me my mission is to remain in my hometown."

Later, at mass, Elidé was overjoyed to see the parroco officiating at the altar with great tears running down his face. "How happy I was to see him weep!" she says. "It showed he was really feeling something in his heart."

At the end of the service, the good man came up to her and said, "Elidé, now I understand everything. Padre Pio told me that you must find a proper person to replace you in Sestri Levante, and you must carry on with the mission he has given you."

In 1950, a Genoese woman named Piera Delfino published a book about Padre Pio that he liked very much. "I asked her to come to Sestri Levante and give a lecture on her book," says Elidé. "Sestri Levante was, and is, a Communist stronghold, and I booked a cinema directly opposite the party headquarters to annoy them. We distributed leaflets announcing the lecture, and the Communists rushed around tearing up every one they could find."

But not enough. The cinema was packed, the lecture was a great success and the collection plates overflowed. The sponsors raised fifty thousand lire, with which they bought a bed for the hospital being built in San Giovanni. The Communists, mad with rage, asserted in a letter printed in the newspaper that a famous dressmaker (Elidé, of course) had organized a scandalous lecture about a holy man that was nothing but a pack of lies and a public hoax. On reading this, Piera Delfino's son-in-law summoned Elidé. "Signorina," he said to her, "this is defamation. You mustn't put up with it. We must pursue them."

"Don't worry about it," Elidé replied.

"But it is calumny," he fumed. "Anyway, I want to defend my mother-in-law."

"Go ahead and defend *her*, but don't mention my name. *My* defenders are Padre Pio and our Lord. That's enough for me."

"Well, in the end, it all blew over," she says, "but from then on, we had one success after another."

One day, Piera Delfino wrote asking Elidé to arrange for her to give a lecture in Turin. Elidé, on Padre Pio's instructions, had organized a prayer group in Turin, and she wrote to the head of it about Piera Delfino and her book. "You must fix this up by yourselves, because Padre Pio wants me to go work in his new hospital and I have the *tombola* to organize in San Giovanni." This was a charity lottery she ran every year for the benefit of the hospital.

Obviously Elidé was too busy to leave, but Padre Pio had other ideas. The next time Elidé went to confession, he asked her, "Why don't you go organize that lecture in Turin?"

"But, padre, I am doing the *tombola* here."

"How did he know about the lecture?" asks Christine.

"I have no idea. He even knew I had written to tell Signora Delfino I couldn't make it. He always knew exactly what was going on."

"Well, then," Padre Pio told her, "you go fix it all up; then come back here for the *tombola*. I am praying for you and for her, and rest assured that everything will go well," the padre told her before she left. She was going to need those words of reassurance.

When she met with the members of the prayer group she found them in a state of total confusion, unable even to find a hall for the lecture.

"Listen to me," Elidé said to them. "I don't want just four old holy women to turn up. I want all the smart and sophisticated ladies of Turin. Which is the biggest theater of all?"

"Now, Elidé," they said, laughing, "be realistic."

"Never mind about that. Just tell me which is the biggest and most beautiful theater."

"It's the Carignano, but they will never rent it to you."

Elidé was staying with a friend. When she got back to her house, she tackled her at once: "Signora Poli, I want to take over the Carignano for my lecture."

Around the table sat the nine Poli children, all grown and in solid professions. "Think of me, who left school in the third grade," says Elidé. "What on earth was I doing among all these learned, brilliant young people? I felt thoroughly depressed at the thought."

"Elidé!" they all shouted. "What are you thinking of? They will *never* let you have it."

"Imagine how I felt," says Elidé, "ignorant, and with no money . . ." Then the thought came to her, "This is the devil putting these ideas into my head." At once she felt better: Had not the padre said—?

When the laughing had died down, Signora Poli said, "Listen, the wife of the owner of the Carignano is a good friend. I'll ring her up at once."

"My husband is very sorry," her friend said, "but they never hire the theater out to anyone. If they let your friend have it for her religious cause the Communists will clamor for it, too."

Elidé was very disappointed. Mentally, she reproached Padre Pio: "You said you would help me, and now look what's happened. Where do I go from here?"

Next morning she went to mass and then made her way to the Carignano. "Listen," she told the owner, "I've got to organize a lecture on Padre Pio, and I want to hire this place for it. If you're afraid that you will be plagued by others who want it too, you don't know Padre Pio. I assure you he will never allow any undesirables to bother you."

The theater owner said he couldn't possibly let it go for less than fifty thousand lire, a substantial sum in 1951.

"Very well," said Elidé calmly, "I'll sign for it."

"I didn't have a bean," she tells us, rolling her eyes, "just a few lire my mother gave me when I went off on the trip. At home I earned my money with dressmaking, but that was impossible when I was traveling. In spite of this, I signed for that fifty thousand. Out in the street, I nearly fainted. 'Who has made me do this?' I asked myself. 'I am crazy!' Then suddenly I had an idea: I will send the bill to Padre Pio. He made me come here; he will have to pay." And so, feeling a little more cheerful, she set off for home.

"Where have you been?" they all asked.

"I've taken the Carignano for my lecture."

"How did you *do* it?"

"And when I told them they shouted and laughed and hugged and kissed me," says Elidé.

She then showed them the paper she had signed.

"For God's sake, Elidé! What are you thinking of? Where will you find the money?"

"I will send the bill to Padre Pio and he will have to pay. He told me to do everything as well as I could. Now he's got to pay for it."

"They all hooted with laughter at this," says Elidé. "They really thought it was the greatest joke."

Suddenly Elidé remembered a wealthy friend, a marchesa, to whom she had once given up her precious confession ticket. She telephoned her, and the marchesa offered to give her twenty-five thousand lire at once.

"If you give us twenty-five thousand lire, we are almost home," said Elidé. "For the rest I will pass the hat around."

"I will see what I can do among my friends," said the marchesa. Hardly an hour had passed before she was back on the telephone to say that she had the fifty thousand lire.

Posters, leaflets and tickets were needed, so Elidé went to a printing shop her friend recommended, where the woman in charge said to her, "My contribution will be all the printing you need."

After distributing the leaflets by car with Signora Poli, Elidé went to see her prayer group and told them what she had done. For a moment everybody was speechless with astonishment. Elidé then gave them their instructions: "During the intermission, you will circulate through the theater collecting contributions. Two of you will stand by the door to sell the books.

"Eventually," she continues, "I telephoned Piera to tell her I was coming to collect her."

"'I'm sorry, Elidé,' she said, 'but you can't come. My confessor has forbidden me to give this lecture.'"

"I went quite mad with rage and horror," says Elidé. "See how they put sticks between the spokes of my wheels at the last minute!" she exclaims to us. "See how difficult it is to work for Padre Pio! You really have to be strong and determined, and never give in; otherwise you can never achieve anything.

"I had to convince her. 'Signora, do you realize what I've done? You've heard your lecture advertised on the radio. *Now* what are you doing, making a fool of me like this! You must come, or I will put someone else in your place.'"

Elidé had no idea whom she would get to speak in the author's place. It was pure bluff, but she was desperate.

"Elidé, do you realize whom you are talking to?"

"I am talking to someone who understands nothing."

Piera was shaken. "At least wait until tomorrow morning," she pleaded.

"Either you are here tomorrow night, or someone else will be."

In desperation, Elidé thought she might even have to go on the stage herself. "Padre Pio will put the words in my mouth, I thought, but I was shaking like a leaf. She kept me waiting until eleven o'clock the next morning. Then she rang up to say 'I've got permission from my confessor. Come and get me.'"

By eight o'clock the theater was full. A central box, the door locked, was reserved for possible eminent latecomers. Elidé stationed herself in the wings in case her star needed anything during the performance. At the beginning of the intermission she went downstairs to organize the collection boxes. Suddenly one of the ladies exclaimed, "Oh, look up there in the box. That's Padre Pio!"

"It *is* Padre Pio, yes, do look. It's him!"

Elidé went down into the pit to look for herself, and there indeed, in the closed box, was Padre Pio himself. Leaning over the edge, with his mittens on, he was stroking his beard and looking around at the audience.

"You see, I had written Dr. Sanguinetti," says Elidé, "telling him to ask Padre Pio to help me, as the devil was giving me so much trouble. So he came, to make sure everything went well."

The lecture proved to be a great shaker-up of consciences. People who had stayed away from church for fifteen or twenty years were now going to confession again. It was a success in material terms as well. The collection came to two hundred and sixty thousand lire, a fortune in those days. And when Elidé went to the manager of the theater to pay the remainder of the bill, he insisted on contributing twenty-five thousand lire himself!

Several pilgrimages later, Elidé was bringing her lambs into the corridor for Padre Pio's blessing when he called out to her, "You are wanted at home."

Elidé was shocked. "My mother is ill?" she asked. But the padre said no more.

Pausing only long enough to commit her pilgrims to the care of responsible persons, Elidé rushed back to Sestri Levante. It was a terrible journey. "I don't know how I got through it, crying all the way," she says. But when she got home, her mother was perfectly well. Elidé couldn't understand what Padre Pio had meant. She planned to stay for a fortnight, and the two women had a wonderfully happy time together. They went for long walks and took trips out into the countryside. One day, her mother said, "You know, Elidé, I feel so happy that even if I were to die now, you must stay with Padre Pio and go on doing good work. My heart is full of happiness."

Halfway through Elidé's visit, her mother had a heart attack. "Every morning," says Elidé, "a Franciscan priest came to give us Communion. My mother was happy that we could take it together, with me kneeling beside her bed. To me it seemed that it was Padre Pio officiating, because the friar had a white beard and was a very good man."

One morning, her mother said, "Last night I dreamed that Padre Pio was at the end of the bed, blessing me. And he breathed on me three times, like the Holy Ghost."

The next day she was dead. She died serene and happy. "She had always asked me to be with her at her death," Elidé tells us, "and after I told her that Padre Pio had promised me he would take care of her, she no longer worried about my constant trips to San Giovanni."

So Elidé went back to San Giovanni, going straight to confession when she arrived.

"Padre," she sobbed, "what am I to do now?"

"Listen to me," he said. "I am now your entire family: mother, father, brother, anything you want. Your mother is in heaven. Let us concentrate on trying to get there ourselves. We must do our best to deserve it."

"He was a great comfort," says Elidé, "and I was happy to stay on and work for him always."

12

PENNIES FROM HEAVEN

ELIDÉ HAS ALWAYS BEEN ADEPT AT COLLECTING money for charity. She organized the *tombola* each year with which she raised half a million lire. "Father Eusebio used to come along and say, 'How beautifully you've done it,' and everybody thought the same; it was always a magnificent affair," says Elidé, her face shining.

People started arriving around nine o'clock to buy tickets and try their luck. By ten everybody had left, and Elidé stayed on to restock the stand and stick on new numbers. Padre Pio always turned up on the first day to give the show his blessing and open it by cutting the tape. One year, a friend sent her a handsome three-color ribbon that Elidé draped across the front of the stand.

"Ask the padre to cut a piece of it off and send it to me," her friend had said to her, but before Elidé could open her mouth, Padre Pio asked, "How big a piece do you want me to cut? Like this?"

"How on earth did he know?" I ask.

"He always knew everything. He walked along the tape with the scissors and cut me a nice big piece."

After she moved to San Giovanni, a play was put on there to raise money for the hospital, and the producer requested Elidé's help. "Anything you like as long as it's not on the stage. My role is to act in real life, not on the stage," she told him. But in spite of her request, she was given two parts. Indignant, she complained to Padre Pio.

"It is for charity. You must do it, Elidé," he said. "Just think of the good you are doing, and you will forget about yourself."

So, much against her will, she gave in. Padre Pio could always talk her into anything.

Quaking with dread, she struggled with her parts, but apparently her efforts were not up to scratch. One day the producer caught her by the arm and said, "Elidé, it's no good, we've got to find someone else." Thankfully, she left. But on her way out, Padre Pellegrino said, "Padre Pio will be annoyed if you leave."

At her next confession, Padre Pio said to her, "You are angry, aren't you? Why?"

"Well, padre, in the play I have to curse the Lord, and the words won't come. I don't want to do it anymore."

"It's your part," he said. "Get that into your head. You're not speaking against the Lord."

"Well, padre, you make sure this dreadful thought doesn't come into my head on the stage, because if it does, I'll just walk out."

"Don't worry. You will do it very well. You will see that the thought doesn't even come into your mind."

"So I went back and he was right. I didn't even know what I was saying; I just talked and got the words out without any trouble," says Elidé, still a little surprised at the thought.

For one of her parts she had to wear a beard, and in the other she donned an enormous hat trimmed with intertwined serpents. As she talked and gesticulated, she squeezed two little pumps, one under each arm: Air, propelled through the rubber tubes under the brim of her hat, made the snakes twist and squirm.

"Are they real?" asked Padre Pio in alarm.

"No, padre. They must be made of rubber," the friars told him, but they were not too sure themselves.

"And who is that?" the padre next asked, referring to the snake-ridden sorcerer.

"It is Elidé, padre."

"Impossible!" he exclaimed in amazement. "And the man with the beard, who is that?"

"That's Elidé too, padre." He roared with laughter. He just couldn't get over it.

Elidé had made a special trip to Turin to buy all the requisite props: the stars and moon for the sorcerer's cape, the snakes, the little bells to sew onto the cloaks, and, of course, all the fabrics, as there was nothing of the kind in San Giovanni.

"And you made all the costumes?" I ask.

"I cut them out and stitched them after work. Sometimes I was dead tired. The padre sent me a message to take it easy and not get too exhausted."

"How often did you do these plays?"

"Twice a year, on May 5 for the padre's feast day, and on the anniversary of the day he took the habit, January 22. We always put on a new play, which meant a whole new set of costumes. Many people came. The theater was always packed. We made millions," says Elidé.

"*Millions*, in San Giovanni?" I say dubiously.

"Yes, we did. I still don't know how it happened, but we did."

I was not to discover until later how this remarkable feat was accomplished.

When Padre Pio was born, it was the custom in Pietrelcina to take new babies to the astrologer to have their fortunes told. So his mother, who, with her sound common sense, probably didn't attach too much importance to the ritual, took tiny Francesco along. The astrolo-

ELIDÉ (*SECOND FROM LEFT*) BEARDED AND DRESSED FOR AC-
TION IN A BIBLICAL PLAY.

ger told her, among other things, that "A great deal of
money will pass through your son's hands, but he will
never own or keep any of it." And the strange prophecy
turned out to be true, for the padre, all through his life,
collected huge amounts, from various sources, for his
many causes.

It was another of the padre's spiritual daughters,
Margharita, who enlightened me further on the mystery
of how the theatricals could have brought in such impressive amounts in San Giovanni. There were no set prices
for seats, she explained, and each person gave what he
could afford. Two actors collected the contributions in a
handkerchief and gave them to the padre.

"He went upstairs to count the money," says Margharita, "and while he counted he did a little multiply-

ing, after the manner of the loaves and the fishes. There is no other explanation. Everybody saw how little money was taken."

The next morning, as the cast arrived in church, they asked the friar who was lighting the candles, "Do you know how much money we made last night?"

"Yes, twelve million."

Twelve million! The padre *had* to have made the lire increase as he counted them. "We had proof of this later," Margharita says. "The first show had been done for the people of Foggia, and conceivably the contributions could have been substantial. But the next was put on for the local inhabitants of San Giovanni. As they were very poor we certainly didn't expect much from them." And the next morning, the Little Flowers asked the friar, "How much did we make last night?"

"Eight million."

Eight million in San Giovanni! Unthinkable. "So I went to the producer and said, 'Don't you think the padre is working harder than we are?' The producer agreed. 'My sister,' he said, 'it's clear that he is multiplying the takings.' The padre didn't want checks you see, because of the signatures, which meant he couldn't multiply them. Incredible, and yet these are the facts," says Margharita, her face glowing at the memory.

13

THE LITTLE WORLD
OF MARGHARITA

MARGHARITA, WHO COMES FROM BARI, FIRST MET Padre Pio in 1948 after the death of her father, whom she had loved very dearly. The loss had left her emotionally disabled. Her grief, instead of abating with time, grew worse, and she felt quite desperate. A woman she knew suggested that she go to Monte Gargano, where a remarkable friar helped disconsolate people. "Well, why not?" thought Margharita, so off she went to the little town on the mountain to track this friar down.

She thought he would surely sympathize with her sorrow and comfort her in her grief, but Padre Pio didn't see it in that light at all. His mission on earth was not to patch up broken hearts but to reclaim lost souls and repentant sinners. A requirement on which he insisted was the absolute conviction on their part that only divine intervention could redeem them. When they were finally brought to their knees, and often reduced to tears of repentance for their sins, then and only then would he give them absolution and become the kindest and most loving of fathers.

Padre Pio had to work fast. Long, tentative conversions were not for him. Penitents who arrived in a hesitant frame of mind were packed off to mature else-

PADRE PIO IN THE CONFESSIONAL.

where. He only picked the fruit when it was ripe. Each soul processed by him came out stripped, greatly sanctified and already halfway to heaven. Over and over again I have heard people say they came out of that confessional bursting with unearthly joy and walking on air. The people of San Giovanni are nearly all in this enviable condition.

So, full of hope and confidence, Margharita had lumbered up the hill to the little church, to pour her grief into Padre Pio's ear. Disgusted by her self-pity, he had banged the shutter in her face. (To us this may seem harsh, but he knew exactly how to deal with each individual soul—and who are we to judge?)

Poor Margharita, who hadn't been aware of doing anything wrong, went back to her lodgings in a state of total confusion. She had always gone to mass every morning and led what she thought was a very devout life. The people in her lodgings suggested that she wait a week and go to the padre again after thinking things over. This was a special way he had, they said, and she shouldn't worry about it too much.

Acting on this advice, she went back the following week, and this time she merely said her father had been taken from her. This went down much better. After a fairly thorough cross-examination, Padre Pio gave her absolution. From that moment, Margharita lost all wish to go home again. For the first time in her life she felt completely at peace. She was floating in a kind of serene, heavenly bliss—but her funds were running out, and she consulted the padre about it.

"Work and eat," was all he said.

Meanwhile, she needed a place to live, but there was nothing available. In the end, after a long search, she found a one-room hut near the base of the mountain, in the middle of a field, without light, water, heating or plumbing. Margharita had to be up at four every morning to get to mass at five. At that hour, in winter, it was hideously cold. The north wind howled, and blizzards raged over the bare, treeless mountain. As she stumbled across the fields, frosted snowflakes slashed at her face like little razor blades, and the icy blast cut right through her thin coat. On top of everything else, she was terrified of the dark.

Then one morning, she suddenly heard a voice. She whipped around nervously, but saw nothing. "One, two, one, two," the voice was saying. She stopped in her tracks and heard no more, but as soon as she began to walk again, the voice resumed its counting: "One, two, one, two," all the way to church.

"Padre," she said the next time she went to confession, "I am going mad. Now I am beginning to hear voices. They keep saying, 'one, two, one, two' until I get to church."

"Ha!" Padre Pio exclaimed. "It's your angel counting your footsteps to keep you company. It is just to let you know he is there, watching over you on your way."

Soon after that she began to worry about sleeping alone in her hut, miles from anywhere. "Padre Pio, if you really are a saint, do something, help me, *please*," she prayed desperately one night as she lay in her bed, quaking with fear.

The next morning when she opened the door, there was a large and beautiful Alsatian sitting outside, and the two of them set off together. The dog, who seemed to know where she was going, walked ahead. He led her right up to the church porch, then disappeared.

That night, before going to bed, she opened the door a crack and peered out. The dog was curled up on the step, and he looked up at her and thumped his tail. In the morning he was still there, waiting to take her to church. "I didn't feed him. I could hardly afford to feed myself," says Margharita, who now slept soundly at night, watched over by her angel and her dog. Too soundly, in fact, as she could no longer wake up in time for early mass. She spoke to Padre Pio about this, but he made no reply. The next morning, however, Margharita was awakened by a terrific racket. She peered out the window, and there was a bird, singing his little head off. Every morning he repeated the performance, keeping it up until she went to the window, when he would fly off.

Her next visitor was a mouse. She complained to Padre Pio about this surfeit of attention from the animal kingdom.

"Even the animals love you and keep you company,

and you complain," he said. "What are you grumbling about?"

It was she who had asked him if her angel ever turned up when she sent him along with a message, and the padre had answered with his usual sharpness, "Why? Do you think he is as lazy as you are?"

Fortunately she was handy with a hypodermic needle, and for this service she was much in demand at the hospital. But it wasn't always easy to find her. One day, as she was sitting in church telling her beads, she became aware of Padre Pio staring at her. She wondered if she had done anything wrong, but as she had nothing particular on her conscience, she just stared amicably back. "Seeing that I wasn't making a move, he leaned out of the confessional and yelled, 'Go on, get on with your work! What do you think you are doing, sitting there like a great lump?'"

"He means you, Margharita," another woman told her.

"Oh, all right, all right," said Margharita, getting up. "Now I can't even sit in church, minding my own business, anymore!"

On the porch she bumped into a woman who exclaimed, "Margharita, where have you been? We've searched for you everywhere. Please come quick. We need you urgently." At that time Margharita was doing private nursing.

Eventually she was given a job at the hospital. Offered a three-year contract, she foolishly signed it without reading it first, only to find herself tied to night duty six times a week. She felt she had been trapped into this. From now on, for the next three years, everything was to go hopelessly wrong for her. What she didn't know at the time was that Padre Pio had fixed up this program of repeated disasters to speed up the sanctification of her soul.

Most of the other employees were earning between eighteen thousand and twenty-two thousand lire a month. Margharita complained to Padre Pio. "What does it matter to me," he said heartlessly. "I am concerned with your soul, not your body." And then he added ominously, "Prepare yourself for the cross which the Lord is sending you."

After three years of working all night without getting enough sleep in the daytime, Margharita was in a state of nervous exhaustion. In despair she went to see the treasurer of the hospital, who coldly reminded her that she had signed a contract.

"But that was three years ago," wailed Margharita, "and I am still getting only fifteen thousand lire a month!" As the treasurer remained unmoved, she announced that she would simply not turn up for work anymore. This had the desired effect, and her schedule was changed so that she would work for two weeks during the day, followed by four weeks of night duty. After sampling this new regime, she felt better, and life began to look up again.

One day in 1959, Doctor Kisvarday was brought into Margharita's ward unconscious. For three days and nights he lay in a coma. Not long before, Padre Pio had said to the doctor, "Carletto, the Lord has already established the date of our death, but I'm saying a special prayer to add one more year to the time allotted to you."

As the doctor lay unconscious, Paola Novak, his housekeeper, watched over him night and day until she collapsed from exhaustion. When Margharita arrived to take her place, a young nun was sitting by the doctor's bedside. A nearby window was wide open, with the icy wind blowing directly onto the bed. "Sister," said Margharita, "close the window; the patient is in a coma."

The next time Margharita came back to resume her vigil the window was open again. "But, sister, what is this?" scolded Margharita. "If you want some air, go outside. This man is dying."

"Yes, Margharita, you're right," the little nun agreed, and closed the window.

The third time, it was open again. "But, sister, you're out of your mind," Margharita groaned.

"Margharita, to you I can talk," said the nun earnestly. "You see, I'm praying for the padre to come and cure the doctor, and I'm leaving the window open so he can come in that way, because he won't want to be seen coming through the door." (At that time Padre Pio wasn't going out, or even celebrating mass.)

"Sister mine, if the padre comes, he comes through closed doors and windows," said Margharita. "I'm going to get the milk ready in the children's ward. I will be back in a minute." The nun left the sickroom and met Margharita on her way back. Just then they saw a monk leave the room and walk away, and they went in together.

All at once the patient, who hadn't spoken for three days, exclaimed, "Oh, what beautiful perfume!"

"It's the alcohol, doctor," said Margharita, who was preparing the hypodermic for an injection.

"No, no. It's the perfume of the padre. He came. We talked and he left."

A little less than a year after this, the good doctor went to heaven. But he had his extra year of perfect health.

One day, Margharita was asked to start a prayer group in Bari. Of course Padre Pio had to be consulted, and he approved.

So off she sped in a bus. As she was getting off, the bus lurched away abruptly, and down she crashed with all her weight on the sidewalk. There was a loud crack, and when she tried to stand up, she realized her leg was broken. The skin was gashed, and she was bleeding.

She looked up in despair, and there in front of her stood Padre Pio!

At the hospital, they placed her leg in a cast without first dressing the wound. Before long, her toes had gone black and she realized she had gangrene. By then she was beginning to understand the purpose behind her continual misfortunes: "Prepare yourself for the cross. . . ."

But at this point she rebelled. "No, padre," said Margharita. "I was willing to put up with pain if I had to, but I am *not* prepared to lose my leg."

So saying, she slipped a picture of him under the plaster at the top of the cast, then back to the hospital she went. Stretching her out on the operating table, the medics clicked their tongues and nodded their foolish heads. "Yes, yes," they said, "she's got gangrene."

"We will have to cut off your leg," the doctor announced, and ordered the cast to be removed.

"Underneath it, the gangrenous wound on my leg was completely healed," says Margharita. Although the plaster was soaked through with poisonous juices, the skin was smooth and healthy without the slightest sign of wound, scratch or infection. "You should have seen the doctor's face. He was amazed."

As soon as she was back in San Giovanni, she hobbled along to see Padre Pio.

"Padre, thank you for what you did," she said.

"Thank the Madonna," he said. "Don't think about it anymore. Just rest and come back later."

"But what am I to do about this leg? By the time I get to church, mass is over."

As if he knew nothing about her leg, he asked, "But why do you miss mass? Ah, you're afraid of the dogs?" The stray dogs of San Giovanni Rotondo turned up for Padre Pio's mass every morning. Sitting on the porch (animals are forbidden to go into consecrated buildings), they listened quietly to the service without so much as a scratch or a snarl. As soon as it was over, they trotted off in good order and spent the rest of the day minding their own business, hunting, exploring, fighting and carrying on in the usual rowdy manner of semiwild dogs of poverty-stricken areas. (It was presumably a member of this club that had been detailed to watch over Margharita's slumbers and lead her to church every morning before dawn.)

"Are you afraid of the dogs?" he asked again. "Don't worry, I'm here to keep an eye on them."

As Margharita painfully shuffled home, she kept wondering what the padre was talking about. "What have the dogs got to do with my leg?" Padre Pio frequently tantalized his Little Flowers by talking in enigmas. She decided to call on her friend Antonietta, regarded by the sisterhood as the most saintly of them all. A wasting disease had kept her on her back for seven years, and Padre Pio was a frequent visitor at her house. Whenever he was known to be calling, the Little Flowers rushed there to get an extra blessing; but sometimes, for he loved to tease them, he arrived in bilocation, invisible to all except Antonietta.

Margharita, feeling thoroughly fed up, told her: "Antonietta, I'm leaving this place. There's nothing more Padre Pio can do for me."

"Margharita, listen to me. There's nothing Padre Pio *can't* do for you. Last time he was here, an angel came and knelt at his feet. He made some request I couldn't hear, but the padre's reply was quite clear to me."

"What did he say?"

"He replied, 'I permit it,' which means that the angel was asking his permission to do something. So you see, even the angels prostrate themselves before him."

Margharita was not impressed. "So what? Who is he, anyway? Just a priest like any other."

"No. If you really knew who he was you wouldn't act this way. I am telling you this so that you will accept your fate and stay with us here, Margharita."

Gradually her leg grew stronger. And of course she

stayed in San Giovanni, since it was by now unthinkable for her to live anywhere else. The town's powerful spiritual atmosphere had become the breath of life to her. She discussed everything with Padre Pio, who led her, not always gently, ever deeper into the center of her own being, where dwelt the Kingdom of God.

This was all very well up to a point, but she felt she wasn't accomplishing anything. She longed for a heroic, more exalted existence. One day, during confession, she saw blood on Padre Pio's forehead.

"It's the crown of thorns, isn't it, padre?" she asked. "Can't I help you to bear it? Won't you let me do something for you?"

"And what do you think you could do, you stupid creature? Just endure your life a day at a time," he replied impatiently. And then, perhaps to make up for his brusqueness, he added, "Remember that we are in Passion Week," which meant that during those few days his sufferings increased immeasurably.

Once, when she felt she had been obtuse about something he was trying to explain to her, she went back to apologize: "Padre, last time I was here I didn't understand what you meant. I made you suffer terribly."

"And you went off and told everybody about it right away," he said accusingly.

"No, padre," she answered, shocked. "This was something we discussed in confession. It was secret. I didn't tell anyone."

"And yet . . ."

"No, padre, I only invoked the Madonna and the saints."

"So you think it's a small thing to turn paradise upside-down?" And he banged the shutter in her face.

By now Margharita knew a great many people around San Giovanni. One girl she met came all the way from Bologna to book her confession, then went home until her turn came up. As she did this every ten days, a good deal of traveling by train was involved. Young, attractive girls don't go unnoticed in Italy, where men are particularly susceptible to a pretty face and very enterprising into the bargain—and on one of her trips the young Bolognese found herself alone with a railway Romeo in her compartment. "Padre Pio," she prayed, "come and help me quick!"

At this point the ticket collector came in. He sat down in a corner and stayed there until the end of the journey. The girl was much relieved. When she got to San Giovanni, she said to the padre, "You know it isn't always the women's fault when men get fresh with them. Please stay close to me always."

"Isn't it enough for you that I dress up as a ticket collector and keep you company for three hours on end?" he replied.

Another time Margharita was in the corridor waiting for her daily blessing. There was a large crowd, through which a man was pushing with great determination.

"Padre," he bellowed, "my wife has a tumor. I have a lot of children. You must cure her for us."

"Yes, all right, I will pray."

"No, padre, you must cure her at once."

"Don't you know it is easier to cure a tumor than change the heart of a man? Very well," said Padre Pio. "It will mean a little tightening of the belt for the spiritual children—here a headache, there a sore leg, a sacrifice for another—and we will offer it all up to the Lord for your wife's recovery."

The woman was cured by the time her husband got home.

One day, Margharita asked him, "Padre, do you think I should renew my vows of poverty?"

"Certainly, my dear daughter, and tell me, how do you observe the vow of poverty?"

"By being careful not to possess anything and not to waste anything," she answered.

"No," he said, "you are mistaken. It means to keep what you have, but to be detached from everything and everyone."

Now it happened that when Margharita arrived in San Giovanni she brought with her a handsome silver rosary with medals of the saints between the decades. As she told her beads on the hill going up the Way of the Cross, people would come up to her and beg for her beautiful rosary. But Margharita clung to her treasure, even though she knew she should have said, "Here you are, take it."

"As you see, I was not detached," she says, "but I got my lesson."

One day she went to see Padre Pio to ask his permission to visit her cousins in San Marco in Lamis. "As he made no objection, I got on the bus, telling my beads all the way there and back, with the rosary in my hand the whole way. When I got home I went to get the rosary out of my coat pocket. It wasn't there." And although she looked everywhere, even tearing out the lining of her coat, it was nowhere to be found. "I had lost a treasure," she says with no apparent regret. She went to the gift shop, where Signor Abresch, who had started the business many years earlier, presented her with a secondhand rosary that had lost its cross. Accepting it gratefully, Margharita went off to church, where Padre Pio was hearing confessions. "Bless it, please," she said. He looked at it with his head cocked first on one side, then on the other. "I was very pleased that he was taking so much interest. I didn't know he wasn't looking at the rosary. What he was saying was, 'You asked for it. Now do you understand?'" Then he blessed the rosary, and Margharita went off cheerfully, by now quite resigned to the clumsy, ugly old thing.

A few days later, on her way to church, she suddenly became aware of something dangling from the hem of her coat. "Click-click" it went, as it bumped against her leg. She unbuttoned her coat to investigate, and there, hanging on one thread of the lining, was the silver rosary.

Unable to unravel the mystery, she popped in to see Antonietta on her way home.

"What do you think, I've found my rosary!" she announced.

"I know," said Antonietta, smiling. "That's the way the padre licks us into shape. You were very attached to that rosary, so what could he do but take it away from you? When he saw you no longer cared, he gave it back to you."

"I understood the lesson," says Margharita with one of her very rare smiles, "and when the next person asked for it, I said, 'Yes, yes, take it.'" So now Margharita has lost her fine rosary for good, and regards this as the price she had to pay to learn what poverty truly means.

After leaving the shepherd's hut, where she had been attended by the dog and the bird, Margharita shared a small flat with two other girls, but found it as difficult as ever to wake up in time for early mass, until someone thoughtfully set an alarm in the corridor. At last, having managed to save a little money, she asked Padre Pio's permission to buy an alarm clock.

"Well," he exclaimed, "it's about time!"

So Margharita bought a clock. "Listen," she said to one of the girls in the flat, "don't worry anymore about setting the alarm for me in the morning."

The girl looked at her, surprised. "I don't set any alarm," she said.

Margharita spoke to her other flat-mate. "Alarm clock?" said the girl. "What are you talking about?" So it was Padre Pio, again, who had rigged up some system of waking her. "No wonder he thought it was time I got a clock," she says.

Soon after this she had to leave the flat and find other lodgings. But out of her meager salary she couldn't possibly pay rent as well as feed and clothe herself. What was she to do?

"By then Padre Pio was dead, and I could no longer discuss my problems with him. So I went along to the crypt. It's not just his body lying there, you know," she says. "His spirit is around as well." In the old days she and Padre Pio had never minced words with each other, so now she warned him, "If you don't find me a place to live soon, I shall put my stuff on a truck and go back home."

And to us she explains, "I have a habit, when I walk down the street, of saying a prayer for those who lived and died in the houses I pass on my way. That night I had a dream. I was walking down a road, saying this prayer as I went along, when I heard the sound of some-one digging. I stopped in front of a house whose occu-pant had recently died and whose new owner was away. In the garden, bent over and digging weeds, was a monk. As he stood up to straighten his back, he put his hands on his hips as peasants do. And I recognized Padre Pio's hands. He looked straight at me.

"'What are you doing?' I asked.

"'I am doing what the living should be doing,' he answered. 'This is an abandoned villa. Why aren't you doing something about it? Tell Lina it is time she came back to occupy her villa. The Lord needs good strong, generous souls, not feeble, irresponsible ones.'

"'Yes, padre,' I said, and woke up." Margharita sat up in bed, wondering what this dream could mean. She

MARGHARITA IN THE GARDEN WHERE SHE DREAMED SHE SAW PADRE PIO.

wrote to Lina, giving her the padre's message. Around the end of June Margharita saw the windows of Lina's house open and rang the doorbell.

"You know," Lina told her as she let her in, "the padre was quite right, but I don't feel up to living here anymore. I have too many memories of him and my sister. I don't know what to do."

"Why don't you come for the summer at least," Margharita suggested.

"Good idea," agreed Lina. "I will do that."

"Those who have no house have to leave and those who have one don't live in it. Strange, isn't it?" mused Margharita.

"Well, do *you* want to come and live here?" asked Lina. "You could have the two rooms and bathroom upstairs. . . ."

"Yes, that would suit me fine. Thank you."

Margharita went straight back to the padre's crypt and said, "You are a great man. You have managed to find me a house and bring Lina back at the same time."

Since then Lina has returned every summer to her villa, which she always finds well cared for, so Padre Pio doesn't have to come back to earth to pull weeds out of her garden anymore.

· 14 ·

A HARD NUT TO CRACK

TINO, A ROUGH AND VIOLENT MAN, WAS THE COM-
munist leader of his hometown. Religion was
anathema to him, God an invention for women and
feebleminded crackpots and faith the opium of the poor
and underprivileged.

Some of his neighbors, Communists like himself,
kept an eye on his house while he was away at work.
One day, one of them told him, "Tino, there have been
nuns in your house."

"In *my* house? Impossible. Never!"

"Yes, there were."

Next day, to check out this unlikely story, Tino left
work early and went home. Sure enough, he found two
nuns cozily chatting with his wife around the dining-
room table. Raging like a maniac, he threw the terrified
creatures out into the street. Then he beat up his wife
and son to drive the point home.

That night, lying on his bed in a drunken stupor, he
was suddenly awakened by a dazzling light. A bearded
friar was standing at the end of his bed, glaring at him.
"This time you've gone too far," the visitor said, gripping
the bed rail with his mittened hands. "I'm waiting for
you at San Giovanni." The next moment he was gone.

"It was all so real I thought my wife had a lover,"

Tino says. So he rampaged and roared about the house searching for the vanished figure, while his wife, in tears, tried to explain who the visitor had been.

Christine describes Tino as a short, determined, grizzled little man, pugnacious but very simpatico. I can picture him standing on his short, stout legs spread wide apart, his hands in his pockets, and a puzzled, doubtful look on his face.

"Did you realize you were behaving badly?" asks Christine.

"No, I was convinced that the Party was right, and that I was living correctly. I didn't need God, but I was always in a state of agitation, always finding some excuse or other to get out of the house. That was in 1949."

On the morning following the apparition, Tino questioned his wife. "Who was that friar?"

"It was Padre Pio," she said.

"Where is he?"

"Near Foggia. In San Giovanni Rotondo."

"How do you know him?"

"I went to see him without telling you. I went with Marista."

Marista was a holy woman who lived nearby and who often saw Padre Pio in bilocation as well as in San Giovanni. "Then," Tino told Christine, "I understood why I felt so uncomfortable in our bedroom. She had stitched a photograph of the padre inside my pillow! Well, after that I just didn't enjoy life anymore. I was bored with everything, even the cinema. I didn't find it fun any longer, behaving like a pig. I just wasn't myself anymore."

One evening, he said to his wife, "Let's go find this friar of yours. You round up some people to share the expenses of the journey, and we will pay him a visit." The woman was delighted. Among the friends she collected was the good Signora Marista, who was frequently employed by Padre Pio for rescue operations of that kind. Three days later, on a fine spring morning, the little group set off for San Giovanni.

As soon as they arrived, all of them except Tino filed into the little church. Remaining outside on the piazza, he looked around in growing astonishment. The atmosphere was totally different from that of his hometown. People walked about quietly with rosaries, there was no shouting or blaspheming, and even the men chatted together amicably. Tino felt like a fish out of water. "I just couldn't take all this mealymouthed stuff," he says. "I just couldn't stand it."

Eventually Tino entered the sacristy, where he found a crowd of people milling about. "From which door does Padre Pio come in?" he asked someone. "Straight ahead. He will be here in a minute," he was told. So Tino planted himself at a safe distance, facing the door. As soon as the padre appeared, Tino recognized him.

"So, the mangy old sheep has arrived," said Padre Pio at once. Everyone was asking, "Do you hear? Who did he say this to?"

"Who is the mangy old sheep?" asked a man standing next to Tino.

"Oh, go take a walk. What do I care who he said it to?" snarled Tino, knowing perfectly well who Padre Pio had in mind.

Three days later he went to confession.

"Oh, so you were a Catholic Communist?" asks Christine.

"No, no, but it was the only way to speak to him. He didn't even give me time to get down on my knees. 'What do you want from me?' he barked.

"'I've come to confess.'

"'I don't want to go to hell for you. Confess to somebody else and come back in two months' time.'

"And he threw me out," says Tino. Incensed, he

went to one priest and then another, but he couldn't bring himself to go through with his confession. "I couldn't swallow the fact that Padre Pio refused to give me absolution. If hearing my confession meant he would go to hell, it must be the same for the other priests." Tino felt totally confused. He longed to get everything off his chest, but he couldn't bring himself to do it.

"Let's go home," he said to his wife, finally. The woman was in despair, all her hopes dashed to the ground.

But at the bottom of the mountain, he stopped the car. "I want to speak to Padre Pio," he told his wife. "I must know which one of us is right." So back up the track they drove.

This time the couple stayed four days, and Tino decided to put Padre Pio to the test. He had heard women say it was enough to ask for graces mentally during mass, as the padre picked up everything from the air; so one morning at mass, he asked, in his head, "some ugly things," whatever they may have been. When the service was over, Padre Pio tapped him on the head, saying, "It's not true what you're thinking, ignoramus. Go and learn the Ave Maria."

Tino was even more perplexed than before. He had also heard a woman say, "It's enough to go to the graves of Padre Pio's parents and ask them for what you want." So, without telling anyone, he trudged off to the cemetery. As he didn't know any prayers, he lighted two candles, one for each parent, and said to them, "You are the parents of Padre Pio. Tell him to accept me, also. I would be glad to have a kind word from him. And tell him that I would like to be accepted by Jesus, too." From there he went back to the friary and into the corridor, where he dropped to his knees, like everybody else. As he didn't want to be conspicuous, he kept his eyes lowered.

"I saw Padre Pio's sandals pointing in my direction and his cord dangling under my nose, so I looked up."

"So, ignoramus," said the padre, tapping him on the head. "This time you've found the right road."

As Tino didn't know how to pray, he bought a little book from which to learn. But it wasn't easy. "I made Padre Pio suffer with my stubbornness. But I really wanted to be convinced of the existence of God," he says.

In the end, after a year, Padre Pio gave him absolution. On the great day, the padre saw Tino rub his hands with joy at being forgiven his sinful past.

"What are you rubbing your hands for?" asked Padre Pio.

"You made me suffer for one long year, padre, and I am happy it is over at last." Padre Pio took him by the wrists. "Do you realize you stretched me out on the cross for the whole of that time? And for you I shed blood."

"You see," says Tino. "That's the way he paid for the absolution which made me so happy."

As for Tino, he didn't really have much trouble giving up his wicked ways. "It was Padre Pio who did everything. I don't even know how I stopped blaspheming, how I gave up sin. But sometimes, in confession, I would say, 'Padre, I can't manage this.' 'Tino,' he would answer, 'you put in the good will, and I'll see to the rest.'"

Tino became more and more attached to Padre Pio. For seventeen years he spent three weeks of each month in San Giovanni and the fourth week at home. Four times a month he went to confession. "Padre Pio gave everything," he says. "His affection overflowed. I had no merit. It's not that he liked only me, but you can have more affection for one person than another. Many times, if I wasn't present at the evening reunions, Dr. X or Professor Y was sent to find me. Padre Pio knew the affection I had for him. But sometimes, as we talked, I would look at him and think, 'Mamma mia, what am I doing here in this friary? The world is so beautiful and here I sit looking at this ugly old friar, with veins all over his face.' And my head would sink down, filled with thoughts of escaping and never coming back. But when I raised my head again, Padre Pio would be transfigured, with a face so beautiful that my soul was close to bursting."

"Tino! What's the matter?"

"Padre, you are so beautiful. . . ."

"Ah, no one has ever said this to me before. But why are *you* saying it?"

"I don't know, padre, it comes from inside here, in such a way that I would like to shout to the whole world how beautiful Padre Pio is."

"Well, well, well."

Wanting to know whether anybody else had seen the transfiguration, Tino asked one of the men who had been present. He told Tino that during the hour they had spent with the padre, his face had changed ten times.

"Changed into Jesus?" asks Christine.

"Yes."

One evening, the disciples were discussing the stigmata. Everybody was asking questions, even Padre Pellegrino, that reserved and self-contained Capuchin, a model among all friars. "Tell us about the stigmata, padre," he said. But Padre Pio said nothing. Then everyone started talking at once. Someone said, "It was the crucifix in the choir that pierced your hands and feet and your side." Each in turn gave his view on how it happened. And still Padre Pio kept silent. Tino thought to himself, "No, it can't have been like that."

"Tino, what do *you* think?" Padre Pio asked him.

"I don't agree with the others," he said. "I think Jesus came down from heaven and embraced you, be-

PADRE PIO CELEBRATING THE 5 A.M. MASS.

cause His wound is on the right side of His chest, and yours is on the left. This could only have happened in an embrace, padre."

"You are closer than the others," was all Padre Pio would say.

Fishing among his Communist ex-comrades at home, Tino brought new recruits to San Giovanni all the time. When members of the Party accused him of betraying the movement, or laughed at him, he would first punch them in the nose, then drag them along to Padre Pio. On meeting the holy man, most of them would turn over a new leaf. John McCaffery describes this in his lively style: "And so it came to pass that month after month he would arrive with a cargo of Reds. . . . And for some time [Tino's] squads became a regular feature of San Giovanni Rotondo. I remember seeing him march off one of his cohorts to the hospital, where blood donors were being sought. 'Boys,' he was saying, 'they need blood and we've got loads of it. Come on!'"

For the Communists, Tino was a menace, a thorn in their flesh. They wanted to lynch him; they threatened him with murder. But the Lord gave him strength to defend himself and stand up to them.

"You are like Jesus," he once said to Padre Pio. "Put the words in my mouth, because tonight they are coming for me." And when, in the end, they did get him, Padre Pio gave him the strength to fight them off.

He was in San Giovanni when Padre Pio died. "On that night he confessed me. I was the last person to be confessed by him. He was slumped down in his chair. I asked, 'Padre, how do you feel?'

"'Worn out, finished. Pray to the Madonna to call me.'

"'Padre, if you go, what will happen next?'

"'You will tell everyone that I am more alive than ever before. And here they will find me, and they can ask anything they like, and I will refuse nothing. I will be better known after my death than during my life.'

"Those are his last words," says Tino. "So, I'm telling you, go to his tomb and put everything in his hands. He is there. He will listen to your prayers and grant you anything you ask."

· 15 ·

THE GOLDEN AGE

GABRIELE, WHO OWNS A SPARE-PARTS SHOP FOR cars in San Giovanni, has agreed to tell us his story. Shy and diffident, like most of the male population of the village, he is relieved to find Elidé in the car when we pick him up at his shop. As they both worked for Padre Pio while the hospital was going up, they know and respect each other of old.

When he was small, Gabriele worked with his father at the bauxite mine halfway down the mountain on the way to Foggia. Father and son used to set off at 3:00 A.M. and stop at the friary's little church to salute the Madonna. Then they would trudge down the mountain in the dark, stumbling along with several hundred other people making for the same destination. When they finally arrived at the mine head, the men went below, while Gabriele and the other boys worked the surface. From morning till night they wielded the pickax, men and boys alike.

Over the years the mine claimed the lives of twenty-eight men, including Gabriele's father.

It was not long after this that Padre Pio launched his appeal for funds to build the hospital. The remarkable squad of helpers he had coaxed and coerced into giving up their own careers and concerns to further his great project got down to work. First of all, the United Nations

139

donation had to be secured. The funds had arrived in Italy, but the responsible officials were extremely reluctant to part with them. Our heroes went to Rome, and within a short time they had unearthed half the sum. They hastened back to San Giovanni and handed the money over to Padre Pio, before heading back to the capital for the second half. And so, with funds in hand, the hospital's foundations could be laid.

The pioneers worked together like brothers. Every evening they reported to Padre Pio on the day's progress and sought his advice about projected activity. As a rule, Gabriele attended these meetings. "If it hadn't been for those men," he says firmly, "the hospital would never have been built."

But of course things didn't always go smoothly. Some architects complained, for instance, that the principal architect, Angelo Lupi, was not a professional, meaning he had no diploma. So he went to Padre Pio and offered to resign. "Nothing doing," said the padre. "You go right ahead. They received their diplomas from men. You got yours from God. I want your work, not your papers."

Another of Lupi's so-called crimes was taking on unqualified labor. He had a golden touch with his men. No matter how unskilled they were, there was nothing he couldn't teach them. Everything was done on the spot. Lime was scooped out of the mountain for the manufacture of bathroom and kitchen equipment. Machinery, which jogged up the mountain on mule-back, was fitted into place piece by piece. A homemade power plant produced electricity. For a steady supply of water he tapped the aqueduct of Apulia.

His extraordinary resourcefulness and his constant presence saved a great deal of money and kept the workmen on their toes. As there was still no transport, he went home to his family only three or four times a year.

PADRE PIO AND DR. SANGUINETTI (*BEHIND THE WHEEL*) AT
THE HOSPITAL BUILDING SITE ABOUT 1950. GABRIELE STANDS
AT THE LEFT OF THE CAR.

Sometimes, when he was lucky, he managed to borrow
an old jeep, but he usually walked—about a hundred
miles—to Pescara.

Living like a hermit himself, sleeping in an old
chicken coop, Lupi didn't coddle his work force either.
Up at three o'clock every morning, he was already hard
at work by the time his huge team arrived on the site. He
had the managers and the laborers take all their meals
together in the half-finished building, through which the
wind howled on its way down the mountainside. However cold the weather, he allowed his gallant crew no
heating whatever. The hospital funds were not to be
squandered on comforts for the builders.

Dr. Kisvarday was in charge of accounts, and he
only let the money out in dribbles. The way he made it
last seems, in retrospect, almost miraculous.

As soon as it was feasible, the doctors opened a first-aid department. Sanguinetti treated his patients free of charge, and night and day he went out to visit the sick.

"Anybody who was ill could always count on him. Those first men who worked with Padre Pio were true apostles. Their goodness shone with light and splendor," Gabriele adds, waxing lyrical at the memory, and I find myself becoming quite misty-eyed at the sound of so much goodness.

"Didn't you work for nothing yourself?" I ask Elidé.

"Yes, for two years I was the unpaid cook: Dr. Sanguinetti bought the food, and I cooked for the whole gang. Everybody ate together, all eight hundred of them."

This golden age lasted for quite a few years after the war. "And then," resumes Gabriele sadly, "everything changed." Once again the church authorities seemed determined to take Padre Pio away.

For a long time now I have been trying to understand the motives behind these recurrent efforts to remove him from his friary, but without success. Everybody tells me a different story. Whatever other considerations were involved—and there surely were others—it seems likely that the authorities were worried that the situation would get out of hand. Too many pilgrims converging on San Giovanni could cause chaos, perhaps even panic and hysteria. Their prolonged presence in an area with such limited sanitary facilities might conceivably give rise to cholera and other horrors, for which the church would undoubtedly be blamed.

In 1960, the famous visitation took place. The good people of San Giovanni were incensed. Their beloved padre was suspected of various irregularities. An inquest was set up, people were interrogated, odious insinuations and allegations were made and calumnies bandied about. Armed with pikes and pitchforks, an angry crowd surrounded the friary. There was a rumor that Padre Pio was going to be whisked away in a helicopter. At once Lupi organized a defense force, posting his men in the trees around the convent. This sight calmed the population's fears for the time being, and, pacified, the citizens went off to bed. But that night another rumor was going round that a Vatican car had driven into the friary gardens, with orders to kidnap Padre Pio, and Gabriele was instructed to investigate. With the help of his friends, he climbed over the garden wall. At once the guard dogs set up a tremendous row.

"I am normally afraid of dogs," he says, "but this time I didn't even think of them, and they stopped their racket at once. I snooped around all over the grounds. I crept into the stables and the garage. But nowhere did I see a Vatican car."

So back over the wall he climbed with the glad news. As soon as he hopped down on the street side, the dogs again gave tongue.

Forty years earlier, when young Padre Pio was first going to be transferred, Gabriele's father had taken part in the demonstrations of protest in 1920. This had been the first time the authorities had tried to transfer Padre Pio. "It's a family affair," remarks Elidé, "from father to son."

Then came the terrible day when Padre Pio died. Gabriele, shattered with grief, went straight from work to the church, where the padre lay in state. All through the night, without food or water, he stood guard; and in the morning, still without eating, he went right back to work. "And I wasn't the slightest bit tired or hungry," he remarks with surprise. At the end of the day he returned to stand beside the coffin again. Even at the funeral he managed to remain beside Padre Pio, staying close to the bier throughout the procession.

"The crowds were enormous," he says. "There must have been a hundred thousand people from all over the world."

· 16 ·

INAUGURATIONS

ACCORDING TO ALL ACCOUNTS, THE DAY OF THE HOS-
pital's official opening, May 5, 1956, dawned
clear, and the sun rose in a bright blue sky. An
altar had been set up in the porch outside the hospital's
main entrance. There, surrounded by fifteen thousand
people, Padre Pio celebrated High Mass.

The ceremony was opened by Cardinal Lercaro, who
had been flown as far as Foggia by the Italian Air Force.
The president of the senate, an old Resistance hand, was
there to represent the government. Dozens of bishops
from all over the world were present, and Communion
was distributed to the faithful by a galaxy of friars and
priests.

After the cardinal's opening words, Padre Pio stepped
up to the microphone. This was a day for which he had
prayed, worked and schemed for many years. Obviously
deeply moved, he first thanked the congregation and his
supporters from all over the world for their help, their generosity and their prayers. "A seed has been sown," he said. "A
new militia founded on self-denial and love is about to rise
for the glory of God and the comfort of the sick. . . . In order
that it may grow and mature, it needs to be nourished." And
he appealed to their further generosity to keep it going.

In Padre Pio's mind, the hospital, which was opening

with three hundred beds, would have to expand enormously. He saw it as one of the most modern medical centers in Italy—with a difference. A true spirit of "militant Franciscanism" would pervade all its departments.

Recruiting the staff for such a project had been no mean task. Only the most exceptional candidates were considered. Outstanding character, integrity and dedication were essential. Padre Pio's team, brought together to hire a crew, conducted a campaign and combed Italy from end to end. It was no easy assignment finding anyone who measured up to Padre Pio's standards. And so many were needed all at once! And yet it was done, and all the vacancies were filled in time for the inauguration day. Today, the situation is reversed—there is a long waiting list of medical staff wanting to work and train in Padre Pio's hospital.

It was not until the clinic really got going as a working concern that Padre Pio's dearest wish finally came true: that the poor people of the area would be properly looked after when stricken by illness and disease. Those destitute spiritual children of his were getting free care at last. It was, really and truly, God's own hospital. The town itself got a terrific boost from its opening. New houses sprang up for the doctors. Shops came into being to cater to all these extra customers, more hotels were built and even the roads were mended! Prosperity came to San Giovanni, up to a point.

For some years all was well, but of course nothing remains the same forever. In time, particularly after Padre Pio's death, the blazing, idealistic spirit of the early days gradually deteriorated. A new, less altruistic staff took over as the original veterans died or retired. A different, less dedicated outlook began to prevail. The initial practice of providing free treatment still holds for the less well off, but those who can afford it now have to pay.

Knowing the place inside-out as Elidé does, she offers to give us a tour of the clinic. This is an opportunity not to be missed, and we jump at it.

This establishment, which would look quite ordinary in a large Western city, is remarkable in the deserted back country where it stands in all its marble glory. When you consider that it was built exclusively with mule and bullock transport, without any local source of either water or power, and financed by charity funds alone, it represents an extraordinary achievement.

Built on noble lines and with grandiose proportions, boasting huge marble staircases and vast terraces, the clinic commands magnificent views over the Apulian plain to the Adriatic beyond. Costly marble of every color is everywhere—on floors, walls and pillars, in halls and corridors. Shocked by this extravagant decor, journalists used to chide Padre Pio about it. "For the sick, nothing is too good," he always replied.

At the foot of the main staircase is a bust of Dr. Sanguinetti, whose death so shattered Padre Pio. John McCaffery says that tears would run down his face at the mere mention of the doctor's name.

"But, padre, you know he has gone to his great reward," McCaffery would say.

"He has, indeed; but, you know, not only the mind, but the human heart claims its share. . . . Well, never did you think you would see Padre Pio reduced to this."

We come to the little chapel. Around the walls are the stations of the cross, carved out of rare wood and presented by Elidé with money saved from her wages. She points out the altar and tabernacle cloths, pale green taffeta embroidered with gold, which she made herself. There are other sets, all in different colors to fit the various feasts of the year.

"I always picked gay colors; none of the somber tones of death," she says. "Nowadays I can't do this sort of work anymore."

THE CASA AS IT LOOKS TODAY.

"This is like a ship," says Christine, as we tramp along endless corridors with windows on both sides. We are on the way to the machine room, where hissing, thumping, throbbing motors control the heating, light and power. We pass a work gang that is building the advanced surgery ward. The men greet her with respect.

As we go on toward "the nest," where newborn babies are kept in tiny glass cots, a sister swoops out of her office like an angry hen.

"Where do you think you are going?" she clucks, and then, seeing Elidé, "Ah, *scusi, scusi,* signorina. I didn't know it was you."

A baby is being dressed in his going-away clothes. With an imbecilic grin on his face the proud father stands by, clutching a feeding bottle. Italians are completely soppy about babies and children.

We come to the main church of the hospital, lofty as

a cathedral, cold as the grave, severe, bleak and bare in the best modern manner. Upstairs in the choir a nun is practicing on the organ.

"She is learning," says Elidé, who knows everything that goes on in the place. The nun, who has never touched a keyboard in her life before, is now teaching herself to play, by order of the superior. Holy obedience!

We reach the nurses' school, a large, airy wing surrounded by terraces. It transpires that Elidé has made all the curtains and bedcovers for the attractive bedrooms of the student nurses. A neophyte guide with the looks of a young Sophia Loren shows us around. Yes, she is very happy here, she says; it is a wonderful place to work in. There is a waiting list of girls from all over Italy who want to train here.

Back at Elidé's house for a cup of coffee, Christine says, "Do tell your glove story." And Elidé is off again.

"Well, it all started with medals. I had bought some I wanted Padre Pio to bless, so I could give them to friends at home."

She was in the sacristy one day when he suddenly came in.

"Padre, wait," she said, on sudden inspiration. And she seized his hand, turning it this way and that to study the way in which the mittens were made. (To hide his stigmata, which he was forbidden to show, the padre wore half-mittens that left his fingers free.) Elidé, who is a genius at this sort of thing, can take in the shape, size and manufacture of almost anything at a glance. From memory, she fashioned a pair of mittens that were an exact copy of the padre's and gave them to Dr. Kisvarday for transmittal.

"Please ask him to let me have an old pair in exchange," she begged.

"He would be excommunicated if he did," the kind doctor answered, but in the end he agreed.

PADRE PIO, HIS STIGMATA HIDDEN BY
FINGERLESS MITTENS.

Next day, when she went to confession and Padre
Pio opened the little hatch, he said, "It was you who sent
me the gloves."

"Yes, padre, and I was hoping you might give me
one of your old pairs in exchange."

"You know perfectly well I am forbidden to give
anything away. But you can have a medal."

"Thank you, padre." Swallowing her disappoint-
ment, she walked around to the front, and he handed it

to her, saying, "This is the weapon which will preserve you from your enemies."

That evening Dr. Kisvarday sought her out. "Just see what the saints get up to," he said. "Padre Pio tried the gloves on and said they were too big in the hand. The wrists and fingers fit perfectly, but you must reknit the hand." He gave her the stained mittens, adding, "Just tell me, how can you possibly adjust the hand without altering the wrists and fingers? I suggest you make him another pair and keep these for yourself."

So she made the new ones exactly like the first. By the time they were finished, fearing that Padre Pio would see through her trick, she was again too nervous to present them. So she wrapped them up and was waiting for Dr. Kisvarday in the corridor when Padre Pio suddenly appeared. As he walked past, he snatched the parcel out of Elidé's hand and tapped the women on the head with it to clear a path through the crowd.

A few days later Elidé received a letter from Dr. Kisvarday, saying that the padre thanked the signorina from Sestri Levante for the mittens, which fitted to perfection.

"And they were *exactly* the same as the first pair," she says with a giggle.

Because Elidé had worked as a dressmaker before she came to live in San Giovanni, Padre Pio, who never wasted anybody's talents, immediately recruited her services for the friary. She made his undershirts, his habits and his nightshirts. Then in due course, back they came for washing and ironing.

"One fine day," she says, "I had an idea. Why not keep one of the old ones as another relic?" Having decided on this plan, she set off to confession in a great state of agitation. Padre Pio would know all about it before she had even opened her mouth. By now she wished she hadn't gone in for such deception, not to say theft. So she invoked the Lord's help, which she always did when in trouble with Padre Pio. (If she felt she had fallen out with the Almighty, she invoked the padre. She always trusted one to back her up when she was in trouble with the other.)

"O Lord," she prayed silently. "Don't let him scold me. I will bring back that shirt; I promise I will. Just don't let him scold me!"

Opening the little hatch, Padre Pio said at once, "So you have purloined somebody else's property?"

"Yes, padre, I did, padre."

"And what is it?"

"A shirt, padre, it's just a shirt."

"And who did it belong to?"

"It was yours, padre." And Elidé burst into tears.

"But, this shirt," he went on. "Did you need it?"

"Oh yes, padre, I did, I did!"

"Very well, then, and what else have you been up to?"

And so Elidé walked on air all the way home. Everybody else, she knew, had collections of the padre's belongings. "They all stole them like I did," she says ingenuously. "People actually snipped bits off his habit with nail scissors as they knelt at his feet in the corridor."

PADRE PIO BLESSING HIS "CHILDREN."

· 17 ·

TRIBULATIONS

To the people of San Giovanni it was of utmost importance to secure Padre Pio's blessing every day. When, for some reason or other, they failed to obtain it, the day simply didn't go right. Those who could, went to confession every ten days, then rushed to the corridor, where they could get another blessing and, if they were lucky, a word or two with him as well. The sick, who lay in their beds and couldn't get to him, were not forgotten either, since he visited them on bilocation. Padre Pio never neglected any of his spiritual children.

Elidé, whose life was now dedicated wholly to the padre's ministry and who was often on the go twenty hours out of the twenty-four, usually managed to get herself an extra blessing—a kind of superspiritual boost—to keep her strength up. Every evening, at the hour Padre Pio strolled in the garden for a short break, she would hurry up the hill to the friary and stand by the garden wall.

"Padre," she would call out, "it's me, Elidé." The rusty lock would squeak and a wooden gate creak open. Padre Pio would bless her, she would kiss his hand, and back she would go to work, happy as a lark.

Then came the sad time in the summer of 1960 when he was forbidden to see anyone. Arriving from the Vatican for his investigations, Monsignor Macari ordered that the padre be totally isolated, but he permitted him to confess his spiritual children once a fortnight. "No," Padre Pio said firmly when informed of this change. "If they don't come every ten days, they lose their indulgences." And so the ten-day interval was reluctantly granted.

"It was a time of great sadness for us all," says Elidé, who told the padre one day in confession how much she missed his evening benedictions.

"You know quite well, my daughter, that they won't let me see anyone," he answered.

"Padre, if you come to the little gate, I will be on the other side. I will look through the keyhole, you will bless me and I will be happy."

"And so every evening, when he went for his walk in the garden, he came to the gate and blessed me through the keyhole. He walked away, then came back and blessed me once more. Peering through the hole, I saw him just as I always did when he used to open the door. It was almost like old times."

"He must have felt completely abandoned," I say.

"He looked utterly desolate, walking around by himself," Elidé says. "He who had always been followed by crowds of people who loved him and who joked and laughed with him as he teased them and pulled their legs in turn."

On the first day of the new restrictions, Elidé went to confession early. Knowing she had to be at work on time, he always took her first.

"I began to cry," she says. "He asked me what I was crying for. I was so miserable I couldn't get a word out."

"Come on," he said, "tell me why you are crying."

"But, padre, we are not allowed near you. We can't even kiss your hand."

"Yes, you can kiss my hand," he said.

A PRISONER IN HIS OWN FRIARY.

But Elidé was so upset she wasn't able to make her confession.

"Listen, I will give you absolution. Don't worry. Offer everything to Jesus. Be brave." But this made her cry all the more.

"Come," he said. "I will bless you."

So she went to the front of the confessional for his blessing. "I bent down to kiss his hand, and suddenly somebody dragged me away."

"Who?" asks Christine.

"It was Monsignor Macari's secretary, standing just behind me. The padre took his hand away, and nobody was allowed to kiss it after that. The secretary, who was also a priest, gave his own hand out to be kissed all the time instead."

"On whose orders was he acting?" I ask.

"Well, Monsignor Macari came from the Vatican, but this was probably the secretary's own idea. It was quite scandalous. People coming from all over the world were shocked at the state of things. There must have been some sort of rumpus, because after a while they allowed us to kiss the padre's hand again, even though he was still a prisoner."

That was the time the rumor circulated that he was going to be whisked away in a helicopter. The good people of San Giovanni took alarm. Clusters of suspicious villagers gathered outside the friary doors to keep watch. In the evening, Padre Raffaele, who was the superior at the time, came to the window and shouted out that Padre Pio had gone to bed, that nobody was going to take him away and that he would stay right there among his people. And so they were reassured and went home. But it wasn't the end of their anxieties. New rumors sprang up, and at once the crowds returned, armed with spades and pitchforks to stand guard on the piazza. One of the foreign ladies who had settled in San Giovanni complained to Padre Pio during confession about the noise on the piazza during the night.

"Well," he said, "if you are kept awake at night, why don't you sleep in the daytime?"

After three years, when they realized at last just how determined the people of San Giovanni were, the authorities decided to leave Padre Pio in his friary. Monsignor Macari departed with his secretary, and peace returned to the worried village.

But all these perturbations had left a mark, and poor

Elidé was more upset than she realized. "Padre," she said to him out of the blue one day, "let me die before you. I couldn't bear the pain otherwise."

"When I am in heaven I will be able to help you more than now," he told her. "And remember that I am your entire family—mother, brother, father, the whole lot."

But when she got home she started to brood on this again. "After all, I left my mother, my family and my friends, and he doesn't even realize I am here," she grumbled to herself. This thought remained with her as she struggled through her work for the whole of the next day. "All he does is confess you, and no more," whispered the Evil One into her ear. And these thoughts depressed her so much that she began to cry again when she got home that night. The next time she went to confession she asked Padre Pio if he really loved her as much as his other spiritual children.

"What do you expect me to do, put your socks on, as if you were a baby?" he asked.

She felt ashamed of herself, but the minute she got home the thought came flooding back into her mind again. It was an obsession. "What am I doing here, wasting my time? Why don't I go home and lead a normal life?" and so on. Thoroughly miserable, her fine serenity gone with the wind, she trudged back again to confession.

"Padre, are you *sure* that you love me as much as your other spiritual children?" she quavered, on the brink of tears.

"Remember," he said patiently, "that I am your father, your mother, your whole family. You can go around the entire world before you find someone who loves you more than I do."

Even this didn't set her mind at rest. Day after day she brooded. Driven by her anguish, she asked the same question again.

"*Ma!*" said Padre Pio, this time quite impatiently. "From now on I will put you among the forgotten ones, and you will see if you are better off than you were before!"

"Padre, don't do that or I will die!" Elidé exclaimed.

"It's the devil who is putting these ideas into your head. Chase him away."

"But, you must help me, padre. You chase him away for me."

But this time, at last, Elidé was finally able to rid herself of her obsession. "Whenever the thought came back, I chased it out. For it is truly the devil's work to torment poor unhappy souls that way."

One day, as she was waiting on the piazza for the doors to open for mass, she overheard several women talking. "I will send my guardian angel to tell him such and such," said one of them. And Elidé couldn't help smiling at the naiveté of these good women, who professed to send their angels on errands to distant friends, expecting them to bring back a reply.

After mass, she went to confession. "Padre, you will always stay close to me, won't you?" she pleaded.

"Not only will I stay close to you, but I will send you my angel to help you, to protect you and bless you."

"I just gasped," says Elidé. "After listening to the women outside the church, thinking them mad, the padre straightened the matter out for me. After that I frequently sent my angel to him with messages and requests, and I always got what I asked for."

To cheer up Elidé during her ups and downs, her brother gave her a television set. She was delighted with it and up the friary hill she went, to share her pleasure with Padre Pio.

To her surprise he turned on her. "You are happy because the devil has got into your house," he snapped. To him, presumably, the incalculable power of television was more likely to be used for destructive purposes than for holy, edifying ends. So he did his best to protect his spiritual children from its insidious influence. There was nothing he could do about it in the rest of the world— that was the Lord's business—but his own province was very much his responsibility.

Elidé was thunderstruck. "The devil! No, padre, I don't want the devil in my house! I will give the set away."

To this he made no reply.

When she got home that evening, she said to her brother, "Listen, when I come home in the evening I have to sew, and I have no time to look at television. It's really wasted on me."

Elidé suggested giving it to their niece, who was about to get married, as a wedding present. Her brother, suspecting nothing, fell in with this plan.

"And so," says Christine drily, as we totter back to her house, avoiding the potholes of the track, "the devil got into the niece's house instead."

"You told me yourself that when Padre Pio took somebody on he roped in the whole family as well," I remind her. "So there is no need to worry about the niece."

Soon after this, Elidé began to have trouble with her legs. She found it hard to walk up and down the hill four times a day, to and from work, as well as up to mass every morning. So at the end of her next confession she asked the padre for permission to buy a car.

"Whatever for?" was his instant reaction.

"Because of my legs, padre. They ache."

He laughed. "But your house is three paces away."

"Padre, if you say yes, I will buy it. If you say no, I won't, because then I know the Lord will cure my legs."

As he made no reply to this, she peered through the

hatch to see what was up. He was staring at the ceiling of the church as if holding a conversation with heaven. She waited.

"All right," he said in the end. "Go ahead and buy it, and be good."

"So," says Elidé, "I bought the car. Then I wanted him to bless it. 'Padre,' I said, 'will you bless my car? And I would like you to touch it a bit in front for me.'"

"Bring it around," he told her. She didn't know how she would drive it into the cloisters. However, at this point, Padre Eusebio arrived.

"Padre Pio told me to bring him the car this morning to have it blessed," she told him. "Will you allow me to take it in?"

"Go, go, take it there and I will come and open the gate for you," he told her. So the little car got its blessing and was "touched a bit in front."

The next day was Sunday, and the father guardian appeared at the small window overlooking the piazza to make an announcement: "Those who wish to have their cars blessed should bring them here to the piazza, because Padre Pio is not blessing individual cars anymore."

"So that was why, you see, he wanted me to hurry." But one of Elidé's friends, who also wanted a car, was refused permission.

"But, padre, you let Elidé buy one and not me! Why is that? It's not fair," she protested.

"Don't you know that to drive a car you have to have your head screwed on properly?" Then another Little Flower, following the trend, wanted to buy one as well.

"Did you ask the padre?" Elidé wanted to know.

"I didn't, because I am sure he would have said no."

"You are very foolish," said Elidé, who always speaks her mind. The Little Flower just shrugged her shoulders and went off to buy her car.

"Well, she drove it around two or three times, and then she ran over a girl and broke her leg. She had to sell the car to pay the expenses," says Elidé.

It would seem on the whole that things go much less well without the padre's blessing.

After Padre Pio's death, things changed in the hospital. Despite Elidé's fierce loyalty and her forthrightness, the old spirit of exalted dedication was gradually eroded and watered down with the arrival of new, less pious workers. One year, the staff went on strike on Good Friday. "It could never have happened when the padre was alive," says Elidé. A poster of the Communist leader Berlinguer, with raised fist, had been pasted on the main gate, and Elidé, needless to say, ripped it off. The staff announced that they would be striking again on May 5, the padre's feast day. She rang up the manager of the hospital. "This is the padre's hospital, not Berlinguer's," she raged. "How can you allow them to do such things?"

"I know nothing of this," said the manager. "You do what you like. It's got nothing to do with me."

"Just doing a Pontius Pilate, in fact," remarks Elidé.

Elidé had, some time before, had a poster printed at her own expense reading "Viva Padre Pio." "You know what I am going to do," Elidé informed the Little Flowers. "I shall go to the hospital at 2:00 A.M., before they arrive, and I'll put my poster there myself. I will bring all my pots in the car and pack them with flowers and place them under the poster.

"So I rang up all my friends and told them to come and help me with the potted plants," she says.

"Be careful, Elidé, it could be dangerous," they said.

"What a bunch of lily-livered cowards you are!" she exploded. "I don't care if they kill me. I shall go alone if you won't come. I will make fifty trips if I have to, and I will go on my own," she declared.

That evening, having heard of Elidé's plans, the hospital staff called off the strike. The prospect of having to face Elidé with her poster, her pots and her ferocity drained them of all courage. She had won another victory over her hated enemy.

GERALDINE AND
FLORENCE

THIS PLACE IS CRAZY," SAYS GERALDINE AS SHE meets Christine on the church porch one morning. "The people here discuss the doings of their guardian angels the way the folks at home talk about their neighbors." She overheard one woman, it seems, tell her crony, "Whenever I send him to Padre Pio with a question, he invariably comes back with the answer." To which the other replied, "I always despatch mine ahead to find me a parking space when I go to Foggia. He never lets me down."

Geraldine obtained her cure *after* Padre Pio's death, and as she is quite happy to tell us her story, Christine has invited her to tea. Joan, Father Joseph's secretary, is also coming with her friends Florence and Robert, and at the last minute an unexpected guest turns up as well.

Heidi, the last-minute guest, who looks about sixteen, has driven all the way down from Lake Constance the day before. It was her first encounter with a photograph of Padre Pio that had set her off so impetuously on the road to San Giovanni. The girl, visibly trembling with some inner distress, is also ravenously hungry.

"Being here is like having a mirror held up to your face," says the girl, "but instead of showing your face, it reflects your soul."

Two shepherds with Geraldine and Joan (far right) in the hills above San Giovanni.

Tom Graves in his book *Needles of Stone* expressed the same idea: "Sacred sites can be mirrors that pick out your flaws, amplify them, and throw them back at you in a way that forces you to do something about these flaws, or go insane."

What flaw can this innocent-looking creature have discovered in herself to put her in such a state? I probe as gently as I can, but she gives nothing away. As soon as she has finished gulping down her tea, she says, "Will you excuse me if I leave now? I'm afraid I am very tired." And off she goes, ravaged and haunted by her secret. Tomorrow morning she will set off on the long drive back to Lake Constance.

Geraldine, on the other hand, says she never wants

to leave this place again. Like Father Joseph, she feels she has come home at last. This is her third visit, and this time she wants to remain. Age twenty-four, and with a halo of short blonde hair around her head, she looks like one of those angels so dear to painters of the Flemish school.

Her first visit came toward the end of a severe illness. She had been at home in Ireland with her widowed mother for the previous two years, immobilized by a nervous breakdown, caused, she thinks, by her working too hard at college, where she had been studying music.

"I had a terrible fear of people," she says. "I wanted to lock myself away. I just would not see a soul except my family. I wandered aimlessly about the house, unable to do anything. Whenever I heard the doorbell, I fled to my room.

"One day, as I was sitting in the kitchen reading," she says, "I had a funny feeling I can't explain. I just felt as if something was going to happen.

"Soon after that there was a knock at the door. On the mat was my aunt, who told my mother, 'I don't want to see you. I've come to see Geraldine.'

"'Well, you know what she's like,' mother said. 'I don't think she'll see you.'

"There I was, just behind her. I said, 'Come in.'

"'You're going to San Giovanni with me,' my aunt informed me."

"Had you already heard about Padre Pio?" asks Christine.

"Only just. I knew about him as I knew about Saint Francis. No more than that.

"My mother said, 'Are you sure you want to go? Don't forget you will be alone among all those people. I won't be there to look after you.' But I told her firmly that I did want to go."

Early on the day of their departure she went to mass

alone. The thought of leaving that evening filled her with dread. But she managed to get through the ordeal, and the next day she and her aunt were in Rome.

"We got on the bus to San Giovanni, and all my horrors flooded back. My tongue would just swell with nerves. Then came the palpitations. Awful, quite awful."

Eventually, the two women arrived in San Giovanni, and the next morning they went to the church. As they entered the crypt and approached the tomb, a strong scent of roses enveloped Geraldine. She had heard about the perfume, but it was still unexpected. From that moment on she felt well.

"You mean you were cured?" asks Christine.

"I can't really say I was cured. I didn't feel bad one moment and marvelous the next. It's difficult to explain."

"How long were you in San Giovanni?"

"Just three days. And when I got home, mother said my face had changed. By then I felt that no matter *what* happened, God was there."

Geraldine went back to college and finished her third year in music. "I was supposed to carry on and complete the course in the fourth year," she says. "And here I am in San Giovanni instead."

"What made you decide to come back?"

"I had written to Father Alessio, and he wrote back saying he might fix me up with a job. Soon after, a job vacancy occurred at the friary. I offered to stay until mid-September, but he said this is a very busy time and he needed me until the end of the month. I told him college started in October. And here I am still! I've never felt so happy and peaceful."

"I don't believe that anybody who comes to San Giovanni is ever the same again," says Florence, who comes from New York. Having been brought up in the Jewish faith, she had a much more difficult and dramatic time of it than most.

FATHER ALESSIO ASSISTED PADRE PIO DURING THE LAST SIX
YEARS OF HIS LIFE.

"I can remember coming down from that church
furious with myself. 'What am I *doing* in this place?' I
kept asking myself. Remember, I wasn't a Catholic."

Florence had read *Padre Pio: The Stigmatist,* by the
American "radio priest" Charles Mortimer Carty, and she
felt she *had* to see Padre Pio, because he alone, she be-
lieved, could unravel her problem and give her some
comfort. When she saw his photograph and read about
him, she said to herself, "If he can do all those things, he
will have the answer to my problem." The fact that the
padre was a Catholic was of no consequence. "If he'd
been a Buddhist monk I would have gone to Japan. If
he'd been the Dalai Lama I would have gone to Tibet. It
was something about that face. Those eyes. That look."

Florence's arrival in San Giovanni in 1963 was not

very encouraging. It was nine-thirty in the evening, and quite dark. "And there I was in my high heels, hobbling along, dragging my suitcase over the stones," she says, rolling her eyes for emphasis. So she kicked off her shoes and ran down the hill full tilt, arriving in the hotel lobby at a fast trot.

"You can imagine how they looked at me!"

By 4:00 A.M. she was standing outside the church. The dawn stampede took her by surprise. Ruthlessly thrust out of the way by the holy women, she saw nothing. As she had never been to a Catholic service before, she had no idea what was going on. When mass was over and the people surged out, Florence was able to move up and have a look at the altar.

At that very moment, Padre Pio was being helped down the steps by two friars. "And there he was in front of me, holding his hand with the stigmata right under my nose. I stared. I was scared out of my skin. I thought, what am I going to do? Suddenly remembering that he wasn't allowed to let anyone see his wounds, I turned on my heel and for the second time *ran* all the way back to the hotel."

There she sat down to think it all out. "I figured perhaps that square space at the altar was where they exhibited him to the people—that he was on display. So I went back again, but of course he was gone."

A woman there who saw Florence standing around concluded that she was looking for an English-speaking confessor, so she went to summon Father Eusebio. When he arrived, he asked Florence whether she wanted him to hear her confession.

"Is it possible to speak to Padre Pio through an interpreter?" she asked.

"Well, he got so mad. 'Out!' he said. 'Out you go! Write him a letter.' We are good friends now, Father Eusebio and I," she says, "but I went down that hill very angry with myself, ready to pack up and leave."

As she sat brooding over a cup of coffee in the lobby, a man sitting a few tables away addressed her in English.

"What's the matter, signora?"

"I wanted to see Padre Pio, but one of the monks told me to leave, so I guess it's not allowed and I'd better go home."

"No, don't go. I will give you a note to one of the friars who is a friend of mine. He will help you."

So up the hill she toiled once more, and again, to her horror, she found herself face-to-face with Padre Eusebio.

"Oh, no, I thought, not you again! No doubt the same thought went through his head as well. 'I'll go,' I said hastily, but he just smiled. 'Oh, it's you,' he said. 'I'll go,' I said again, 'I'm going.'

"'Give me your note and come back tomorrow.'"

The next morning she went to mass, but by now she was beginning to learn, and with persistence and determination she managed to catch a glimpse of the altar during the service. But she did not see the stigmata again.

"I know it wasn't an accident that I saw it the first time. It was intended as a special grace of God."

After hearing mass, Florence decided to pay a visit to Saint Francis and went around to his altar. There were three or four people there as well. "And suddenly there was this terrible noise thundering in the distance. It sounded like a stampede of cattle approaching. I turned to run, but somebody had put a barricade across the way, and we were unable to move.

"Then a great pack of women, four abreast, were heading straight toward me: fat ones, little ones, tall ones. Running at me ninety miles an hour. Oh God, I thought, where do I go? They came to a dead halt outside the barricade."

At this point a little door in the wall opened up and a friar came out, looked at Florence and her companions, and told them to get down on their knees. "But I was taught in the Jewish faith to kneel to no man, only before God." In the end, however, she decided it would be all right to follow the local fashion to avoid giving offense. As she knelt, the door opened again, and in came Padre Pio.

"I looked into his face. Padre Pio walked past a few steps, and I thought, Oh Lord, he's going to pass me right by. And just that fast, all of a sudden he backed up. He turned around and looked at me like I'm looking at you. He put his hand on top of my head. Tears came. I put my head against the wall and I *cried*. Something happened inside me. I've never been the same since he touched me."

But Florence was worried. She couldn't understand why she was constantly in tears. Had she done something wrong? She asked to see Father Eusebio. They walked up the road for a few minutes, and she told him what was on her mind.

"I think I've done something wrong, father."

"I don't think so," he replied gravely.

"Why do I feel so bad then?"

"I'll ask Padre Pio. Come back tomorrow."

The next day he said, "Padre Pio says you must prepare yourself. He says you must read more."

"Well, I thought, he doesn't know how many books I've read. I've read all those books, and I'm not reading any more. Well, do you know, once I got back to New York I couldn't pass a bookstore. It was like a magnet. I had to go in."

And so, month after month, she went on with her reading, sometimes devouring two books a night. But not one of these books felt right; she was struggling with a major problem.

"I wasn't one hundred percent sure that Jesus Christ was the Messiah. That was my big stumbling block. So I thought, I must go climb that mountain again, and if Padre Pio can tell me one hundred percent that Jesus Christ is the Messiah, I just might believe it."

So back she went to San Giovanni. By now she knew the ropes, so she wrote a note to the padre, which one of the friars took to him. Here is Padre Pio's reply: "I am able to be a humble instrument in the hands of God, but I have not the ability to give you the gift of the true faith. This, in fact, is a gift that can only be given by God. Therefore, I will pray that God will grant you the gift of faith; that is, namely, that you will believe that Jesus Christ is the Messiah."

"In other words," says Florence, "he was handing the problem back to me. It was up to me to ask for the gift of faith, so I could believe that Jesus Christ is truly the Messiah. And when this was granted to me, that moment I was born. I thought I was alive before, but no. *Now* I am alive. It frightens me when I think, suppose I had been left? It was really the hand of God that picked me up on the road where I was lying wounded. And I can understand how people come to drink, depression and suicide, because nobody stops for a wounded person. When Padre Pio put his hand on my head I was healed."

· 19 ·

SEVEN YEARS OF HELL

In San Giovanni it is difficult for strangers to distinguish a shop from a private house. I am constantly surprised to see Christine diving through some ancient, dilapidated doorway and emerging with a clutch of eggs, a chine of pork or a loaf the size of a bicycle wheel. The only shops that really look the part are groceries, since they usually display tomatoes, huge watermelons, velvet-skinned peaches and other fruits and vegetables on the pavement outside. It is one of these establishments that Ginesta and her father administer with rigorous and cheerful efficiency, in spite of the fact that papa speaks only dialect and that his daughter's academic achievements are limited, since she was unable to go to school. Paralyzed and almost blind, the girl had to stay at home, so it was her mother who taught her letters. Now cured, she can see without glasses; and although her eyes are full of scars, they function very well. Her miraculous cure is due, she says, to her mother's persistent prayers.

Ginesta is talking to us on behalf of her father as well as herself. "Shall I tell you about papa's confession to Padre Pio?" she asks.

"Sì, sì," says Elidé, who is interpreting as usual.

"Well, poor papa was plagued by lustful thoughts.

Bad, really bad ones. He couldn't get them out of his mind, and he was too ashamed to confess them. These terrible thoughts tormented him all the time. In the end he forced himself to go to Padre Pio and said, 'Padre, I have lustful thoughts that won't leave me in peace for a moment. What must I do?'

"'Well,' said the padre, 'how can this be your fault? If one of your daughters comes to mass here in the friary and some ruffian or other leaps out of the bushes and jeers at her, how can she be blamed for it?' Padre Pio gave him absolution and said, 'Go in peace.'"

Going home down the hill, the good man asked himself, "What does this mean?" And bit by bit, as his thoughts churned slowly around in his head, he came to understand that just as his daughter would not have been responsible for the lout's actions, so he could not be blamed for the thoughts that plagued him. Greatly relieved that there was no sin on his conscience, he went in peace as he had been told to.

The grocer always went to Padre Pio's mass and never did anything without consulting him. He had borrowed money to build a house for himself and his family. But the interest on the loan was high, and he found himself slipping ever deeper into debt. Finally he took his worries to the padre.

"You know what happens when someone has gangrene?" Padre Pio asked him. "They cut off the affected limb and the patient recovers. But if they didn't cut it off, the disease would spread and the patient would die. So sell the house, settle your debts, and then you can eventually buy the house back in due course."

A woman came to look at the house, liked it and bought it, and Ginesta's father paid off his debts. But as the years passed he longed to have his house back. The buyer was prepared to sell it to him, but only at a much higher price. And besides, he had unmarried daughters to worry about.

It was during this period, a difficult time for the man, that Ginesta had a dream: Arriving at their shop in a taxi, Padre Pio went in and talked to Ginesta for some time. Then he got back into his taxi, cranked the window down, and called out, "Ginesta, come here, come here." She went up to the car. "Ginesta," the padre said, "tell your father that it is my responsibility to look after you and your interests. That includes the wedding and the future. I will see to everything you need. It's no use his worrying. You must tell him."

Shortly after this the woman who had acquired their house needed money to buy a farm for her daughter who was getting married. Ginesta's father, who had added to his savings, was able to buy his house back at a good price, without the burden of a high-interest loan.

"But if you didn't obey Padre Pio's commands, you were in for a bad time," Ginesta says, launching into a new story.

Her sister Maria is a very clever girl. Her headmistress wanted her to go to a university, but she herself had no wish to do so. Maria went to see Padre Pio. "I am now a qualified teacher," she told him, "but my headmistress wants me to go to a university for another four years. I don't want to go on studying, padre."

"My daughter, be satisfied with what you have. Don't go to school anymore," he said. Maria went home delighted. But against his advice and her own wishes, she was nagged and bullied into it, and eventually found herself at the university in Bari. Instead of four years, it took her six to get her degree. During that time she met a young man who was later to become her husband. Maria asked Padre Pio about her Antonio; "Well, why not?" he said. "Is he a good boy? Is he religious?"

"I don't know, but I think so."

"If he is a good boy, go ahead, it's all right," he said.

But Maria said nothing to her father. He was very

strict, and his daughters were afraid of him. If they had anything to ask, they first approached their mother, who then waited for a good moment.

One day, as Maria was walking to church, Antonio stopped and gave her a lift in his car. A sour soul, eager for trouble, saw her get into Antonio's car and rang up her father. Maria never thought twice about it, but the father, when he heard, took a very different view of the matter. "All hell broke loose in the house," says Ginesta. "We didn't eat, we couldn't sleep. Poor Maria couldn't even speak. She felt totally confused. Padre Pio had said, 'Why not, if he is a good boy,' and then, pandemonium."

At that time, Sancia, Ginesta's other sister, had a dream. She was kissing Padre Pio's hand, and he said to her, "Well, haven't you got something to ask me?"

"Padre," said Sancia, "what must I ask you?"

"How is it that you have nothing to ask me?"

"But, padre, I don't know what I should ask you!"

And then, for the third time, he said, "Is it possible that you are not asking me for anything?"

Just then, the family situation blazed up in her mind. "Ah, this is what I have to ask you! It is about Maria. Please help her, because at the moment life at home is hell."

"Yes, this is what I was waiting for. All will be well in time, but for the moment you must wait."

"And we had to wait seven years, every one of which was pure, unmitigated hell," concludes Ginesta.

After seven years Maria got her degree and became a schoolteacher, as Padre Pio had advised her to be, not a professor. She and Antonio were married, and the irate father forgave his daughter's "trespasses."

Christine's last word on the story is that if you ignored Padre Pio's advice, you always had to pay for it in a big way.

20

DOROTHY'S LONG QUEST

THE CASA IS A RELIGIOUS MAGAZINE PRODUCED BY the hospital and edited by the modest and saintly Pio Trombetta, who wrote about Padre Pio under the pen name Gherardo Leone. Dorothy, who works on the English version of the publication, speaks four languages perfectly. She is the sort of person you might well expect to meet in some vast international setup like the United Nations or UNESCO. With her exotic air, her delicate features, her camellia skin, her explosive energy and her lively, inquiring mind, you can't help wondering how she came to land in a barren wilderness like San Giovanni Rotondo tucked away in one of the most desolate parts of Italy. She is coming to dinner with us tonight, so we are about to find out.

"I never push anything," she says, as we settle down in the drawing room with my notebooks and tape recorder. "Whenever something is difficult, I know it is not for me. I realize it is the will of God and I let it go."

Dorothy used to believe in reincarnation. It was the only way she could explain to herself the tribulations of this life. For several years she traveled around the world, trying to find out where she had lived before and who it was who had given meaning to her life. Altogether, she visited fifty countries, but nowhere did she seem to belong.

"When I was in Guatemala, I remember reaching out my arms and saying, 'Oh, I love you, love you, love you,' but there was never anybody there." She had no idea who it was she loved so much.

"I always had in mind the story of the little boy who was told that if ever he found a pebble that felt warm to the touch, that would be the stone of happiness. All through his life he searched for that stone, until he became so impatient that when he found it, he chucked the warm stone into the sea by mistake. So I thought I must always stop long enough to make sure the stone isn't warm." With her search for the truth ever at the top of her mind, Dorothy had a go at everything.

When she first arrived in Guatemala, she went to see a medium who became her "spiritual mother." This lady did all she could to enroll Dorothy in her spiritual cult, but somehow she could never manage to get her to a séance. Dorothy firmly believes that the Lord was watching over her all along and protecting her from the clutches of the devil.

"You see," she says, "this medium was spiritually very powerful."

"You mean she was a witch?" asks Christine.

"Well, she had bilocation." At which Christine and I stare at each other in disbelief.

"Oh, yes," says Dorothy, "the devil is very powerful. Don't forget he still has the powers of an angel. These are no less effective because he uses them for evil purposes. He can give these powers to his followers and teach them his own tricks whenever he likes."

After this she joined the Rosicrucians. She told them her life was useless and that she longed to find a goal. Just the sort of person they were out to net, in fact.

After a course of instruction, they informed her that the time for her consecration had arrived. This ceremony was to take place in a darkened room in front of three candle-lit mirrors. Dressed from head to foot in black, she was then to pronounce the consecration. But she found she couldn't bring herself to do it.

"Did you ever discover who you were supposed to dedicate yourself to?" asks Christine.

"Mirrors always imply witchcraft. In *Snow White* there is a mirror. When you wish to summon the devil you look at your reflection in a glass and call him up." As we shudder at this, she continues: "My morale was low. My spiritual life was agonizing." A Yoga school she had wanted to go to in the Himalayas had been closed because of heavy snowfalls. In Japan, a Presbyterian friend of hers planned to take her to church, but something went wrong. One after the other, every avenue was being shut off.

"One year I spent Christmas at a hotel in New Delhi. After the festivities I moved to the YWCA, which was cheaper. Now I realize that I was *directed* there in order to meet a woman called Maria, who was staying at the hostel and who talked incessantly about Padre Pio and showed me his photograph. Before I left, we agreed to meet in Benares."

Although Dorothy enjoyed listening to Maria's stories of Padre Pio, she didn't really care for the woman herself and decided to push on to Benares two days early. In Benares, which was overrun by pilgrims, she had a good deal of trouble finding accommodations. Eventually she was offered a double room for which she agreed to pay full price, as she wanted above all else to be on her own.

On leaving the room, Dorothy saw the hotel manager coming toward her along the corridor. "Imagine my surprise when who should be behind him but Maria. She had also come two days early, in order to avoid *me!*"

Of course there was no other way. Maria had to have the second bed, and the two women went around like twins, visiting temples, watching the rites on the Ganges at sunset, sailing on the holy river and always talking about Padre Pio. They parted once more and Dorothy thought this time it was for good.

Two months later, Dorothy was in Hong Kong. As usual, she had made no reservations, but in the end, after a long search, she found a room in Kowloon. As in Benares, there was Maria tripping down the corridor toward her!

Some years before, Dorothy told us, Maria had fallen in love with a man who then left her. In her anguish one evening she decided to take her own life. She got hold of a bottle of pills, smashed it with a hammer to get it open, and then, after swallowing the pills, she cut her wrists with the jagged glass. She wasn't found till four the next afternoon. She was whisked off to the intensive-care unit, and there she lay in a coma for a week. When she came around, she had lost all her faculties. Taking pity on her, a friend drove her to San Giovanni. As soon as Padre Pio spotted her in the corridor he blessed her, and she instantly came back to life, regaining all her lost powers.

Maria's story and the image of Padre Pio stayed with Dorothy, and eventually she found herself in San Giovanni Rotondo. The day she arrived was beautifully clear. Although the weather was dry, a rainbow of dazzling splendor sprang from the top of the mountain behind the friary, arching across the sky all the way down to the plain of Foggia below.

"For me this was a heaven-sent sign, a symbol of the Pact of Alliance of the Bible," she says.

Next morning, running with the holy herd, Dorothy managed to secure a seat near the altar at Padre Pio's mass. "As he came in, I was transported into another world," she says. "There was a sudden movement of air around me, with gentle breezes blowing in from all directions, and I was in another dimension. Voices, which seemed to be in my chest, were speaking. I was listening to a dialogue, which ended with the words 'He cannot be wrong.' After I heard this sentence, I knew with absolute certainty that I had found the truth. It was the end of all anguish. I *knew* I had reached my goal at last."

The next step for her was to give up her own will. "I would now say that our ego is the burden of the devil. But mine didn't die altogether that day. There was still a twitch or two in its tail," she says ruefully.

Dorothy's first experience at confession was a disaster. No sooner was she on her knees in the confessional than Padre Pio packed her off, saying her dress was too short. As this was patently untrue, she realized he was using it as an excuse. It was only later she found out that she had done all the wrong things, overdressing, applying careful makeup and lashings of perfume, and so on.

Dorothy was terribly deflated. But one of the friars lent her a long, dark coat; and wrapped in this, with her feet in flat-heeled shoes and a black scarf over her head, she presented herself again, and this time Padre Pio heard her confession. From that moment, knowing that she had found her spiritual home at last, she decided to remain in San Giovanni. Being obviously competent, she had no trouble finding a job—the Hotel delle Grazie put her in charge of accounts. At times there was so much to do that she was working until three in the morning, to be up again by four to get ready for early mass. As a result, she often fell asleep in church. Owning up to this hideous sin in confession, she implored Padre Pio to give her the grace to stay awake during his mass. "When you fall asleep, stand up," he told her. "And if you go to sleep again you will fall down, and then you will wake up, ha, ha, ha."

Another time she arrived for confession in considerable distress. "Padre," she sniffed, almost in tears. "I had three hairs of your beard which I kept as a precious relic. And now I have lost them."

A chuckle came from the other side of the hatch, but no reply.

"Padre," she persisted, "I am very upset. Now I have nothing of yours. Can I do a novena for some of the dried blood off your hands?"

"Yes, go ahead," he said.

(Padre Pio's wounds had to be washed and dressed several times a day, and everyone competed for a drop of his holy blood.)

When the novena was over she went back to the confessional and put out her hand to receive her prize.

He didn't budge.

Dorothy was working for Abresch at the time. All that morning she went about her tasks with a heavy heart, sighing so pathetically that her kind employer asked her what the trouble was. When she told him, he disappeared into the back of the shop and returned with a piece of blood-soaked gauze from the padre's chest wound, which his son had scrounged from the cell one day.

With a pair of scissors, Abresch snipped off a corner of this precious relic and handed it to Dorothy. "And here it is," she says proudly, showing us the locket hanging from a chain around her neck. Beneath the glass can be clearly seen a spot of astonishingly bright red blood.

And now Dorothy is getting ready to leave. "Don't go yet," I plead. "Tell us more tales. I'm sure you've got reams more."

"Well," she says, relenting, "do you know Tina Sartori? She came from Pescara and worked here as a cook in a doctor's household for a while."

As Dorothy tells it, Tina wasn't much of a cook. One day she had to serve chickpeas, but she didn't realize that they had to be soaked overnight and cooked for several hours.

The master of the house was expected home for dinner after a few days' absence, and Tina surveyed her disastrous dish with a baleful eye. What was she to do? In her panic, she invoked Padre Pio: "Quick, padre, do something!" she prayed. The family sat down to dinner, and Tina handed around her platter of grapeshot with a thumping heart.

"Well," said the doctor, "I've never tasted such tender chickpeas in all my life!"

"So you see," says Dorothy, "nothing is ever too small for Padre Pio. All you have to do when trouble strikes is ask for his help. 'Just pray,' he used to say. 'I am not deaf, you know.'"

"Then," continues Dorothy, "there is a story about a group of French pilgrims who brought with them a very clever priest."

This man's problem, it seems, was that he felt quite dead inside. The daily mass he celebrated meant nothing to him. "You wait and see," said his friend, "when you go to Padre Pio's mass, everything will be different for you." But this didn't happen. For this poor prelate it was just a mass like any other.

A few days passed, and just before the pilgrims were due to leave for home, they went to the corridor to receive the padre's blessing. As he walked past the group, he said to the priest, "Give me your breviary." And the priest, thinking Padre Pio was going to sign it for him, handed it over. A certain amount of concentrated scribbling went on, then the priest got his book back. On the front page he found written out the solution to a very complicated problem in algebra that he had been trying to solve for years. This at last had the desired effect, and the priest's deadly indifference melted like snow in the sun.

"You see," says Dorothy, "when people were in good faith, he always found a way of reaching them."

He could also shake and shatter those with evil in their hearts. A man once came here with his wife, planning to kill her on the way home down the mountain. The narrow roads there, twisting along precipitous ravines, make a murder of this kind only too easy to pass off. Who could say it wasn't an accident? When Padre Pio walked into the sacristy where the pilgrims were assembled, he shouted out, "There is someone here with blood on his hands." Then he walked straight up to the man, roaring at him, "Assassin, assassin!" The would-be murderer fell on his knees in tears and experienced a complete change of heart.

At this point Christine brings tea, and we give Dorothy a chance to swallow a few sips before pressing her for more stories.

"And now I shall tell you just one more story, then I must go home," she says. "One day a woman brought her deaf-mute child to the corridor for the padre's blessing. As he walked past, she said desperately, 'Padre, my daughter is deaf and dumb. . . .'

"'No, she's not,' he answered, and the child cried out, 'Mama!'

"The mother was ecstatic. Impulsively, she snatched the gold chain from around the child's neck and pressed it into Padre Pio's hand.

"When she got home she poured the whole story out to her husband. He turned on her in a rage. 'How dare you give him that chain. It was *my* present to the child; you had no right to give it away.'

"So that day, which should have been such a joyous one, ended in tears. But the next morning, when the ungrateful man woke up, he found his property returned to him, lying on the night table beside his bed, intact."

PADRE PIO IN HIS SEVENTIES.

21

THE CROWN OF THORNS

O N MY LAST DAY IN SAN GIOVANNI, FATHER Joseph telephones to offer us a private viewing of the BBC film about Padre Pio. The movie is admirable except for the soundtrack, which has gone to the dogs. The commentary is almost inaudible. Hard as I try to hear, I can't catch more than a word or two, and I resign myself to a dumb show. But the camera team has done a splendid job, and much of the photography is haunting. The hooded figure of Padre Pio in the chapel, immersed in prayer, is right out of the Middle Ages. Shots of the friars strolling along the cypress avenues of the garden exude timeless peace and serenity. And on their way to matins down the interminable corridors, they look like ghosts from a time long dead.

In spite of this ethereal appearance, the Franciscan order is very much alive today. The friary of San Giovanni is a hive of activity. Padre Alessio's office is constantly full of pilgrims in search of books and pamphlets on Padre Pio. The church is packed throughout the day, and there is nothing muted or subdued about the happy worshipers. I once heard the father guardian, who was trying to get his mass going, bellow at the congregation, *"Pace e bene. SI-LENZIO!"* On another occasion, when one of the younger friars was celebrating mass in the chapel, he had to seize the microphone and fire off an equally vigorous volley of commands to temper the voluble enthusiasm of his flock.

Cecil, who spoke at length in the movie, is an old friend of Christine's. Although I couldn't hear a word he said, there is still one hope for me: I will fly to London and get the story straight from the source.

To look at him, over six feet tall and bursting with vitality, you would never guess that Cecil is a mystic. By profession he is a biochemist, with heraldry and genealogy as lifelong hobbies. In the late fifties these subjects became a full-time occupation when he was invited to start a school for family-history studies in association with the University of Kent.

"I have been trying for about seventeen years to write the story of my relationship with Padre Pio," he says as we sit down to dinner. "But it is very difficult. I don't mind telling it, although it's a bit embarrassing. And, of course, it's terribly un-British." We both laugh. I know exactly what he means.

"I seem to remember you had an accident," I say by way of encouragement.

"Yes. I suppose it all started in 1955," he says. "I was in Italy on behalf of the Heinz Corporation, as a quality-control chemist in the tomato fields. My job was to examine the produce, check that it was up to Heinz standards, and see it packed and shipped off to London. It was a very bad season. The crops were damaged, the tomatoes split, and I was on my own to inspect sixty factories, which produced the pulp and juice. For three days and nights I hadn't put my head on a pillow. I slept in the car, woke up and drove on."

One evening, as he got back to his hotel, looking forward to a good night's rest at last, he found a message: there was trouble at the Pontinuri factory. So back he had to go; but on the return trip, so exhausted was he that he fell asleep at the wheel. At a bend in the road he crashed into a stone bridge.

"I thought I was dead," he says. "And although I was aware of debris scattered over an enormous area, I was in a state of perfect, blissful peace."

Rammed halfway into the crumpled gas tank, Cecil thought he was in heaven, surrounded by a serene landscape of rolling hills and distant mountains, all light and tranquility, everything perfectly peaceful and wonderful. "Words won't describe . . . I can't think of anything to compare it with," he says. The damage he had suffered was as yet unknown to him. His shoulder blades were broken, and his arms and legs were fractured in several places. There was a great wound in his head and his rib cage had been smashed in. Altogether he was a mess.

When he came to, he was lying in a hospital bed. The door of his room opened and in came a bearded Franciscan friar, who ordered him to make his confession. But Cecil wasn't in the mood for that. He had no wish to see the old mud raked up, particularly in the state he was in. Gently but firmly the friar insisted, coaxing distant, long-forgotten sins to the surface. Curiously, he seemed to know more about the patient's past than did Cecil himself. And when it was all over, and he had received absolution and Communion, he felt like a newborn baby, absolutely scrubbed. The priest then gave him the last rites, and as Cecil floated away on a blissful cloud of peace, he lost consciousness once more. The next thing he remembered was the arrival of his old friend Marquis Bernardo Patrizzi, the representative of Heinz in Italy and the man who seven years before had brought Barbara Ward to San Giovanni Rotondo, inspiring her to obtain the critically important UNRRA grant toward the construction of the Casa.

As soon as it was thought safe to move him, Cecil was driven to the airport to be flown to London. With his severe concussion, he should never have traveled, but it would be seven years before he discovered this.

Cecil has strong feelings on the subject of suffering. "Analysts," he says contemptuously, "describe the joy of suffering as masochism. It is nothing of the kind. You are simply feeling that inner happiness of sharing the divine possession of your soul." According to him, the human soul is like a block of rough granite, very hard and unimaginative in its structure. "God wants to make that raw chunk of stone into a perfect image of himself. Like any other sculptor he gets hold of his hammer and chisel and goes bang, and whoof, off goes one corner. Well, that doesn't hurt very much; then bang, goes another corner, and so on, until he gets down to finer details. And that's where it begins to hurt. If we can imagine our soul being like that block of stone, we're all being formed into the image of God through suffering," he explains.

"What Padre Pio is trying to get through to us is that God made the soul, that hunk of granite, absolutely free to tumble down the mountain and knock off its own chips. But if it allows the Creator to do the molding, that is, by handing its will over to God, then the soul will be made into His image, and be worthy of heaven."

"There must be an awful lot of wasted souls tumbling down the mountain!"

"Not at all. We can't judge what happens to other souls. I am sure that a lot of people who appear thoroughly unpleasant have some inner qualities that God will preserve."

"Well, let's hope you're right."

Ever since he can remember, Cecil has been powerfully drawn to the life of the spirit. "I want to try and express the feeling I have growing, growing all the time, of the presence of God. Even in hectic, high-pressure business meetings, He is present, and I ask myself if I am really promoting His glory, and what Christ would have done in my place."

"Good Lord!" I exclaim, thinking of some of the businesspeople I know.

"Why do you say 'Good Lord'? It is perfectly normal. My life is pretty intense. The telephone never stops ringing. But as soon as I put it down, I take a deep breath and I'm back with God."

Whatever he may say, Cecil is clearly no ordinary businessman.

When he was home in London again, patched up and feeling fine once more, a strange thing happened. One evening on the underground as he was leaving the car, he suddenly blacked out, and the doors closed on his neck. Another time he passed out at the top of a flight of stairs and crashed to the bottom. These blackouts multiplied and were invariably followed by the most excruciating headaches. "It got to the point when I drove myself straight into the Thames," says Cecil, "and there, to my shame, I got stuck in the mud. It was rather embarrassing trying to explain how it had 'accidentally' happened."

"You were ashamed to admit you blacked out?" I ask, missing the point.

"I wanted to kill myself. The pain in my head was getting more and more unbearable."

Various doctors experimented on Cecil with quantities of pills. They put him through abreaction and hypnosis and kept him awake for a week. Nothing helped; in fact, his condition worsened drastically. He started to have fits, during which he smashed up his house and abused his wife, children and neighbors, but as he passed out after these fits, he never knew about them until he was told. Marquis Patrizzi came to stay with him in England at this time and was present during one of these rampaging scenes. Much disturbed, he decided to take his friend to Italy, and they flew back together, with Cecil in agony all the way.

In Piacenza, Bernardo locked Cecil up in a flat and called the doctor, who took all Cecil's pills away. For the next few weeks he went through withdrawal.

"The agony never left me," Cecil says. "It started at the top of my spine and went around and through my head like red-hot claws of steel. When it was really bad I would bash my head against the wall. I would scream, writhe on the floor and kick out wildly. I was sick over and over again. Then I would collapse for hours."

In the end, however, he was free of his dependency on drugs, and Bernardo laid on a magnificent lunch in Florence to celebrate. Even though Cecil was still in terrible pain, he managed to enjoy it. When the splendid meal was over, Bernardo announced that they were going to visit a friend of his, and they set off to Foggia. Cecil objected that the trip was a waste of time. But his friend was determined to see him cured.

Strangely enough, many of the people I talked to while researching this book started off by saying, "We arrived in San Giovanni in a snowstorm and it was bitterly cold." Those are Cecil's very own words now. Of course, he still had no idea where he was, and why he was there.

The next morning Bernardo called him before five. Cursing and grumbling mightily, Cecil threw on his clothes and staggered down the stairs. He was propelled straight outside into the snow. It was pitch dark and appallingly cold. They struggled and slipped up to the church as best they could, blinded as they were by the blizzard. Cecil had never seen such an enormous crowd for mass before. "What on earth is going on?" he asked. "Is it something special?"

"Wait and see," said his friend. "Just stick to me." And he pushed his way up to the big doors.

When Cecil finally got in, letting everybody go first like the true-blue English gentleman that he is, all that was left was a seat at the back. "The noise was indescribable," he says. "I never heard such a row in all my life. At last an elderly priest came in and started to say mass. Before I realized what was happening, I was completely, overwhelmingly mesmerized. Here was Christ on the cross, dripping with blood. You were really present at the Crucifixion. I was totally engrossed.

"I had sometimes been very impressed by the—horrible word—*performance* of individual priests. But I'd *never* had this experience of witnessing Calvary. I was utterly overcome."

At the end of the service, Bernardo came to collect him and dragged him off, dazed and bemused, to the sacristy. As the priest walked past them, Cecil did a double take. "Bernardo," he said, "that's the friar who came to see me in Piacenza."

"No, no, he hardly ever goes out of this building."

They queued up for the blessing. Padre Pio came walking through the men, and when he saw Bernardo he gave him a great hug and a kiss on both cheeks. "Typically Italian," says Cecil with a grin.

"This is my English friend," said Bernardo. "Get down on your knees, go on. This is the silly ass I told you about who threw himself out of his car."

"'Hmm,' said Padre Pio, as he banged me three times on the head. And the pain vanished, just like that, and I felt *completely* refreshed."

Later that day they went back to the friary and met the padre again in the common room. They began to talk of this and that, including politics. Although Padre Pio never read a newspaper, he seemed to know what was going on everywhere. Then he addressed each man present in turn, asking him about his family and his particular problems.

"Now, this may sound a little strange," says Cecil, "but I still have no idea whether the padre was speaking Italian or English. And although he kept up the conversation with the rest of the room, he was talking with me. He informed me that on the ninth of July my wife would have a daughter named Elizabeth." (This came to pass as foretold.)

"And apart from that, we had a conversation which frightened the daylights out of me. I don't know if it is prediction, or what I am to expect, but to my mind it is the explanation of the constant presence of God. I am convinced that what he told me *is* true. Now, I know I have all the choice in the world. I can go this way, or that way, or any other way I like, but this conviction pulls me back all the time. And I've got to be prepared for it, because in a way it is simply too terrible, and in another way, it just isn't believable.

"Padre Pio made me visualize Christ's agony in the garden, with all its horror and revulsion," he says. "He made me understand the extent of the pain and anguish, the price of sin and of saving souls. He showed me what the Crucifixion cost God—as far as any human being can grasp its magnitude."

When the two friends returned to Piacenza, Cecil tried to telephone his wife in England, but got no answer. Northern Italy was in the grip of frost, and all flights had been canceled. He left by train and arrived in a snow-covered south of England on Christmas Eve . . . to an empty house! His wife had gone off with the children to stay with her brother.

Cecil got into his car and started off across the frozen countryside to retrieve his family. When he finally reached his brother-in-law's house, his wife refused to see him. The situation had become impossible for her; she had decided she simply did not want to go through all that misery anymore. The whole of the next day Cecil spent praying in the local church. His wife came in and, not knowing he was there, went into the confessional.

"On Boxing Day," says Cecil, "we were together again. She had received a telegram, and this is the strange thing about it: it didn't go to our house in Canterbury, but to her brother's in Purley."

"From Padre Pio, I presume," say I, with a rare flash of perspicacity.

"Of course. It said, 'I present to you the Christ Child. I assure you that Cecilio is better. And I grant that all the crosses of your life will be a bouquet of roses!'"

There followed several years of close association between Cecil and the padre. Once or twice a year Cecil went to San Giovanni. Whenever a problem cropped up, he sent a guardian angel to Padre Pio, and quick as a flash, he could see a solution. Again and again, whenever he needed strength, consolation or encouragement, he got a whiff of that fantastic perfume, a reminder that Padre Pio was around.

In May of 1966, when the padre's health was beginning to fail and Cecil was in San Giovanni with Bernardo, the two of them were summoned to the cell on several occasions. Even though his bronchitis was getting worse, the padre loved having men around and enjoyed teasing them. He embraced them, cuffed them and pulled their legs in turn. "Although he could sometimes be wild with anger, there was tremendous warmth in him and a great sense of fun," says Cecil.

On one occasion, when Padre Pio was receiving his flock to bless packages, prayer cards and so on, suddenly there was a furious roar. All heads whipped round. There was the padre, shouting and waving his arms at a terrified little man clutching a parcel. "Open it up!" he bellowed. "Open it up!"

"But, padre," wailed the man, "it's been so carefully wrapped. . . ."

"Open it up! *Open it up!*"

The man reluctantly unwrapped his parcel, and Padre Pio began to pull things out of it, tossing them in all directions. Books flew through the air, holy pictures fluttered to the ground, even a rosary flashed and jingled on its way to a distant corner. It was Christ overturning the tables in the temple all over again.

From the bottom of the package, the padre scooped up a handful of lottery tickets. Furiously, he shredded them to ribbons as he thundered, "Get out! Get out! Devils, all of you!"

"Of course, everybody was very embarrassed," says Cecil with a broad grin.

Another time when Cecil was in the cell, Padre Pio took his hand and just held on while he talked to Bernardo, who soon said it was time to go. "I was about to get up, but the padre pressed down on my hand to keep me there. I looked into his eyes, and for a moment we gazed at each other." Then, all at once, Cecil broke down.

"Padre," he implored, "isn't there something I can do to help you? For seven years I suffered. Couldn't I carry your crown of thorns?"

But the padre just shook his head no. Cecil insisted. "I *must* help you. You can't carry it alone." It was no good. "He shook his head again, patted me on the cheek and went on holding my hand, I've no idea how long. Eventually I got up and left. There was blood on my hand, and the whole of that corridor was filled with perfume, an exquisite, absolutely overwhelming scent."

As a scientist, Cecil knows that scent lasts only a moment until the olfactory glands become saturated and then paralyzed by the perfume. "As you know," he says, "when you put on scent, very soon you can't smell it anymore, although other people still do. But this scent was with me all the time."

They went back to Rome that day. The following

morning, at twenty-five minutes to six, Cecil shot bolt upright in bed with the most agonizing pain in his head. "A pain I hadn't had for years," he says.

"The crown of thorns! My God, you'd been asking for it!"

"Wait a minute. It was really paralyzing pain. It started every morning at five-thirty and lasted for about five minutes." When he got back to England, his wife said, "So you're back in the trouble again! . . . "

"And she would say the rosary while I writhed in agony and banged my head on the floor. As soon as it was over, I was fine, as if nothing had happened at all."

In May 1968, he was back in San Giovanni on his biyearly visit. As he knelt at the consecration of the Host, the pain suddenly hit him again. "No! No! No!" he yelled at the top of his voice. People turned and then looked away. Accustomed as they were to all kinds of maniacs, possessed souls and the like, they didn't pay much attention. He went around to the sacristy afterward, but Padre Pio just sailed past him. There was no pain the following day at mass. The padre briefly smiled but otherwise ignored him, and they exchanged only a few words. Cecil went home, but he had no more pain until one night in early fall.

On September 22, his wedding anniversary, Cecil and his wife had gone out to dinner and then came home and went to bed early.

"At about twenty minutes to midnight," he says, "I was once again bolt upright in bed, with the most *excruciating* pain. Within a few moments I was writhing on the floor, screaming in absolute agony, vomiting, banging my head on the boards." His wife gave him painkillers and cold water, massaged his neck and wrapped his head in wet towels, but nothing helped. Finally she said, "It's him, isn't it?" as she gripped his head in her lap.

"This went on until twenty-five minutes to two, a hell of a long time when you're in absolute agony. And

PADRE PIO'S LAST MASS, SUNDAY, SEPTEMBER 22, 1968.

then, suddenly, there was the most exquisite peace. Absolutely fantastic. With tears gushing from my eyes, I said, 'He's gone.'"

In the morning Bernardo rang up from Rome. "Don't tell me," said Cecil. "Padre Pio died last night."

"You heard the news?"

"No. But I knew."

Padre Pio had died peacefully, said the medical report. And the strangest thing of all is that the wounds in his hands, feet and side had healed and completely disappeared, without leaving the faintest scar.

The last thing he had said to Cecil was, "I promise you I shall not let God take me to paradise until I know that all my spiritual children have been saved." "My own guess," says Cecil, "is that in that hour and a half he went into hell. And I just helped him a little bit."

"But why do you think he went to hell? Was he suffering in advance for the sake of those spiritual children who wouldn't make it to heaven on their own?"

"Yes, I think so, to beg Christ and say to him, 'Look, I'm prepared to do this, to share my suffering with you on the cross to save these people, if they want to be saved.'" And this large, robust-looking, athletic Englishman was roped in to help with the salvaging operation. . . .

"And that is the end of my story," says Cecil, "except that since then I've been able to communicate with him and ask favors."

"Favors?" I ask.

"Well, through just saying a prayer to Padre Pio. I do the praying, and Padre Pio does the rest. Prayer *does* work," Cecil says with a broad grin.

· 22 ·

SWEETS FOR THE
CHILDREN

To those who don't know San Giovanni, the phrase "the perfume of the padre" means nothing at all. But down in the crypt, around his tomb, it is perfectly normal to hear people whisper to one another, "Have you had the perfume today?"

"Yes, three times already."

"Oh, I've had it four times!"

At one time or another practically everybody in San Giovanni has experienced the extraordinary scents that emanated from this holy man's person during his lifetime and that still waft around from time to time.

People who were closely connected with the padre during his lifetime—such as John McCaffery and Cecil, men of the world though they are—accept the phenomenon without question. I must confess, however, that until I experienced it myself, I was totally skeptical about this aspect of the padre's aura, which he himself described offhandedly as "sweets for the children."

The first time it hit me was in Christine's kitchen, as she was trying to describe the scent of Padre Pio's wounded, bleeding hands.

"It is kind of spicy—you know, cinnamon, cloves, cumin and so on."

"You mean all those things you put in Christmas puddings?"

"Exactly."

"Who ever heard of blood smelling like Christmas pudding?" I thought to myself, while trying to keep a politely interested expression on my face. And all at once a very strong smell of Eastern spices bloomed under my nose.

"Good heavens!" I gasped. "I can smell it!"

A minute later it was gone, but in that short space of time it was like being in one of those narrow little spice shops in an Arab *souk*.

Since then it has struck again twice, both times in the south of France, during the winter I spent writing this book. On both occasions my spirits had sunk below zero at the thought of my inadequacy for the task and my lack of qualifications, beginning with the fact that I had never even met Padre Pio.

It was a mournful, soggy day in early spring, drenched in a thick cloud that rolled slowly in among the fruit trees like some monstrous, all-devouring amoeba. Depressed beyond measure, I decided to take a break and go pick the last few sprigs of mimosa in order to bring a little cheer into the house. Paddling about in my gum boots, I shook a few branches free from the sodden mimosa trees—and suddenly the whole garden was suffused with an overpowering smell of spices. The orange and lemon blossoms, which I first suspected of being responsible, hadn't as yet emerged from their thick, waxy buds. Next I glanced at the foot of the old fig tree, where early shoots of lily of the valley stood closely swathed in their glistening green armor, like an army of tiny, tightly rolled umbrellas. The aroma clearly didn't come from there, either. As for the irises, they were still folded up inside their transparent, papery husks. Pointing a questing nose in all directions, I suddenly realized that it came from *everywhere* and nowhere. At last I understood—sweets for the children. . . .

Not long after this I found myself listening to a radio program that shed light on the mystery. A panel of

French scientists were discussing a phenomenon known as the "odor of sanctity." It seems that certain extraordinary states of being, such as intense love, or ecstasy, can cause a breakdown of the fatty tissues of the body, and this chemical change produces the exquisite scents that emanate from certain very saintly persons and from their bodies after death. To die in the odor of sanctity is no euphemism. When the bones of shipwrecked Marys from the Holy Land were disinterred at Saintes-Maries-de-la-Mer in the Camargue, the most delicate flower scents came wafting out of their sepulcher. But Padre Pio, as far as I know, is the only holy person who actually *lived* in the odor of sanctity. He is also unique in having been able to send this odor across the world, both in his lifetime and since his death.

The last time the phenomenon occurred was early one morning after a long, wakeful night fraught with doubts and hours of negative thinking. As I opened the front door to let the cat in, the most overpowering smell of cumin smacked me square in the face. Was I hallucinating? This time I wanted to be certain. I called out to my husband.

"What is it?" he asked crossly as he shuffled down the corridor in his robe and slippers.

I drew him to the open door and waited.

"What a curious smell," he said, sniffing suspiciously.

"What do you think it is?" I asked.

"Pretty funny kind of cooking going on somewhere. Do shut that door, you're letting all the heat out," he said.

So he could smell it too. I now knew for certain it was no hallucination. Sweets for the children . . .

I closed the door and went in to make breakfast.

A CHRONOLOGY

1887   *May 25.* Born to Grazio and Giuseppa Forgione, farmers, at Pietrelcina, near Benevento. The next day is christened Francesco.

1903   *January 6.* Enters Capuchin monastery at Morcone to begin year of novitiate. Takes name Pio in honor of Saint Pius V, sixteenth-century pope and patron saint of Pietrelcina.

1904   *January 22.* Takes provisional vows of poverty, chastity and obedience. Transferred to Sant' Elia a Pianisi for further studies.

1905   *January 18.* First experience of bilocation. Later sent to San Marco la Catola to study philosophy.

1906   *April.* Returns to Sant' Elia a Pianisi.

1907   *January 27.* Takes final vows of poverty, chastity and obedience. Sent to Serracapriola to study theology under Padre Agostino, who becomes his confessor and confidant.

1908   *December 19.* Ordained to the minor orders.

December 21. Receives first major order of the subdiaconate.

1909   *January 18.* Receives diaconate, becoming a deacon.

1910   *August 10.* Ordained a priest at Cathedral of Benevento. Next day celebrates his first mass at his home church in Pietrelcina.

September 7. Shows puncture wounds in hands to parish priest of Pietrelcina, Don Pannullo, but after prayers the wounds disappear.

1915   Obtains permission to stay at Pietrelcina for health reasons. Replies to inquiry of Padre Agostino confirming that he has received visible stigmata and testifies that they were made invisible at his prayer. Also reveals he has undergone crowning of thorns almost weekly for several years.

November 6. Is called up into the Italian army as Private Francesco Forgione during the First World War and posted to Naples as medical orderly.

December 18. Sent home on account of illness to convalesce for one year.

1916   *July 28.* Arrives at San Giovanni Rotondo for the first time.

December 30. Furloughed on six-month sick leave.

1917   *August 19.* Returns to army in Naples.

November 5. Furloughed on four-month sick leave.

November 12. Returns to San Giovanni Rotondo.

1918   *March 5.* Returns to army in Naples.

March 16. Diagnosed as having double pneumonia, he is medically discharged and returns to San Giovanni Rotondo.

August 5. Has apparition of a celestial person who hurls a spear at him.

September 20. Has the same vision, and finds himself with the visible stigmata. Nine days later his fellow friars, alerted by his blood-stained bedding, become aware of this phenomenon.

1919   With the end of the First World War, word of the stigmata spreads throughout the world and pilgrims begin arriving in San Giovanni Rotondo. Church authorities take note of this.

May. Examined by Dr. Luigi Romanelli at the behest of the Capuchin order.

July. Holy Office sends Dr. Amico Bignami to inspect the padre's stigmata.

Fall. General Curia of the Capuchins has Dr. Giorgio Festa examine Padre Pio.

1920   *March 24.* Pope Benedict XV sends his own physician, Professor Bastianelli, to examine the stigmata in company of two Capuchin archbishops.

1922   Soon after ascension of Pope Pius XI (February 6), Holy Office launches an investigation of

Padre Pio. Thereafter, he is forced to offer mass at a different and unannounced hour each day, and forbidden to bless crowds, show the stigmata or speak of them or answer letters from laypersons, and is deprived of Padre Benedetto as his spiritual advisor.

1923   *May.* His proposed transfer to northern Italy is foiled by an uprising of the people of San Giovanni Rotondo. Finally, new orders from Rome permit him to stay.

1924   *July 24.* Holy Office takes official stand proclaiming uncertainty as to supernatural origin of Padre Pio's stigmata.

1925   As a result of Padre Pio's appeals, Hospital of Saint Francis comes into being with two wards and free treatment.

1929   *January 3.* Mother, Giuseppa, dies.

1931   *June 11.* Padre Raffaele, father guardian at Santa Maria delle Grazie, receives communication from the Vatican: while Holy Office is investigating Padre Pio's wounds, the public will not have access to him.

1933   *July 14.* Pius XI restores priestly rights to Padre Pio.

1938   *August.* Earthquake strikes San Giovanni Rotondo, leveling Hospital of Saint Francis.

1940   *January.* Padre Pio proposes construction of a large modern hospital to Drs. Sanvico, Sanguinetti and Kisvarday. Later, in response to Pope Pius XII's appeal for groups of faithful to unite, he gives impetus to a movement called Prayer Groups.

1946   *October 5.* Society for the Relief of Suffering legally constituted.

October 7. Father, Grazio, dies.

1947   Establishes first prayer groups.

1948   *Summer.* British economist, conservationist and humanitarian Barbara Ward visits San Giovanni Rotondo and secures UNRRA grant of $325,000 for construction of the padre's hospital.

1954   *September 9.* Dr. Sanguinetti dies.

1955   Dr. Sanvico dies.

1956   *May 5.* Home for the Relief of Suffering ("the Casa") formally dedicated and opened.

1957   *May 5.* On first anniversary of the Casa, Pius XII names Padre Pio director for life of the third order at Santa Maria delle Grazie.

1958   *October 9.* Pius XII dies, and is succeeded by John XXIII, whose first apostolic blessing is on Padre Pio.

1960   *July 29.* On behalf of Pope John XXIII, Monsignor Carlo Maccari arrives at San Giovanni Rotondo to conduct investigation of Padre Pio and his ministry. They leave September 17, with another persecution in force.

August 14. Dr. Kisvarday, last of Padre Pio's medical team, dies.

1963   *June 3.* Pope John XXIII dies, and is succeeded by Pope Paul VI, who rejects all accusations against Padre Pio.

1965   *May 14.* Padre Agostino dies.

1968   *September 20.* Fiftieth anniversary of the appearance of Padre Pio's stigmata.

September 22. Celebrates High Mass, 5:00 A.M.; confesses men, 8:00 A.M.; blesses his tomb, 9:00 A.M.; blesses the crowd in church, 6:00 P.M.

September 23. Padre Pio dies at 2:30 A.M.

PHOTO CREDITS

The author and publisher wish to thank the following for kindly supplying the photographs reproduced in this book:

Charles Abercrombie: pp. 7, 40, 42, 43, 45, 46.

Christine Abercrombie: pp. 12, 15, 79, 129, 147, 164.

Archives of the friary of Santa Maria delle Grazie: pp. ii, 3 (Padre Giacomo), 9 (Foto Michele), 10 (Padre Rocco Tummolo), 48, 51 (Padre Rocco Tummolo), 167.

Casa Abresch, San Giovanni Rotondo: pp. viii, xiv, 58, 64, 83, 113, 116, 137, 141, 149, 152, 155, 184, 196.